Mindfulness Brings Clarity

BY MEGAN MCKERNAN

Dedication

This book is for MMC and CVP, my two angels in heaven who did not get to live to see their 30th birthdays.

CVP, thank you for teaching me so much about life, even in your death. You are one of the most selfless and kind people I have ever had the pleasure of working with. Seriously, who else finds out they have leukemia when they are donating blood to the Red Cross? I will try to take your advice by not sweating the small stuff and taking the vacation. #LFG

MMC, I'm so glad you contacted me when I was meditating back in June 2022. The journey to discover your story has been nothing short of transformative. They will never erase your existence, no matter how hard they try. I hope I am making you proud.

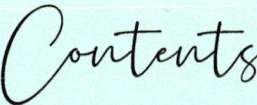

Contents

**Chapter 1: What is Mental Health? Why is it so
Important?** 1
What is Mental Health? 1
Why is it so Important? 2
Mental Health and Trauma: How are They Related? 4
Common Examples of Traumatic Events 5
Post Traumatic Stress Disorder (PTSD) and C-PTSD 7
The Modern-Day Trinity: Mind-Body-Spirit Connection 9
Spirituality:How it impacts the Mind/Body Connection 14

Chapter 2: How does Trauma Come Into Play? 29
The Mind-Body Connection 32
Systemic and Generational Trauma 35

Chapter 3: Mindfulness 40
What is Mindfulness? 40
Defining Mindfulness vs. Meditation 42
Types of Meditation 43
Why Mindfulness is so Important 45
History of Mindfulness and Meditation 49
My Mindfulness Experience 50

Chapter 4: How to Apply Mindfulness to Your Past 57
Eastern Influence of DBT and Other Therapy Practices 61
How to Apply Mindfulness to Your Past 64
Letters to Yourself 90

Chapter 5: How to Apply Mindfulness to Your Present 95
Everyday Mindfulness Techniques 98

Chapter 6: How to Apply Mindfulness to Your Future.....109
Mindful Exercises: Training Your Brain to Craft Your Future..... 120
Creative Visualization Exercise 121
Letter to Your Future Self 125

**Chapter 7: So, Mental Health, Mindfulness...
               What's Next? 128**
Be Kind to Yourself 129
Practice Radical Acceptance.. 129
Bring Open-mindedness and Commitment 130
Get Started with Mindfulness... 130
A Beginner's Quick-Start Practical Guide to Meditation........... 134

Acknowledgements 141
References 145

What is Mental Health?
Why is it so Important?

What is Mental Health?

Mental health is composed of present moments alongside the accumulation of past experiences. It is how our brain responds to the challenges we face and how these experiences influence our mind, physical health, and even personality. In my view, mental health embodies the mind-body-spirit connection in its realized form.

While this perspective is gaining recognition, it's not yet mainstream. Although mindfulness and holistic practices may be increasingly popular, they are often misconstrued with more superficial trends, a sort of "new age yoga" culture. People can easily skate the surface without gaining a true understanding because this interconnectedness between mind, body, and spirit is far from new. It is an ancient understanding that modern science has only begun to scratch the surface of. An understanding that highlights the deep connection between our mental and physical health.

Why is it so Important?

The discussion of mental health needs to be fully normalized, and for that to happen, we all need to chime in. It's up to each of us to bring mental health awareness into our daily lives. Think about it: how often do you pause to check in with yourself and honestly notice how you're feeling? Do you ever ask yourself why you feel that way? Becoming more conscious of our thoughts and emotions helps us better understand ourselves, allowing us to treat ourselves with more compassion and care.

Incorporating mental health awareness into our routines takes time and effort. It's not easy to be mindful all the time. We all have biases, and each of us navigates different experiences that shape our perspectives in infinite ways. It's challenging work, but it is essential for our overall well-being.

Our minds and bodies are connected in ways only self-awareness can show. We need that self-awareness to guide us through a healing journey to reconnect with ourselves. Being aware is the first step of the process, not the end. Sometimes, it is easy to believe that "there's something wrong with me," and there's no help to fix you. But there is! The interconnectedness of our bodies and minds, and awareness of our mental health, can heal us as fast as we can get drunk. We are not broken forever. We just need mindfulness.

Physical symptoms can be some of the strongest indicators for many mental health-related issues. If you're at the end of your rope and feel you have done *everything* to treat your symptoms, consider that they may be coming from deeper within. Practicing mindfulness can help you to get to the root of your problems and allow your mind and body to flourish.

Being a practitioner for nearly two decades has given me a nuanced and informed perspective on the impact of neglecting mental health, not just from observing others but from my own experience as well. In 2020, the stress I was under facilitated my Crohn's disease, marking one of the toughest struggles I've faced. It's been an ongoing challenge, but the most difficult part has been learning to cope with the stress that seemed to fuel my condition.

During this time, I felt mentally isolated. My symptoms were at their peak, and I had to use the bathroom 6-7 times a day, which made me feel disconnected from myself. I had worked with a nutritionist and tried various medications, including cannabis, for a time, but nothing seemed to work. It wasn't until I started focusing on the deep connection between the mind and body that I began to notice a shift and started feeling better.

As COVID-19 began to recede, I sought out a doctor for IV infusions and explored other holistic approaches to healing my entire body, mind, and spirit. I started attending yoga classes more regularly with my neighbor, and having an accountability partner proved to be incredibly motivating. We made a weekly commitment to each other, and that consistency kept me engaged. The instructor also played an important role in my experience and growing love for yoga, as I was fortunate to have someone who made the classes enjoyable. Over time, I realized that moving my body no longer drained me; in fact, I felt recharged afterward. I also felt happier.

Mental Health and Trauma: How are They Related?

What is Trauma?

Trauma is an emotional response to a severely distressing event. It can stem from many different experiences and affect the mind, body, and spirit. Everyone reacts to situations differently, and your trauma will never be exactly like someone else's. A trauma response can manifest in various ways. If your body has a lingering and distressing emotional response that it cannot regulate on its own, it may be considered trauma. Some people can process an experience and move on, while it's not that simple for others. The response comes from your entire being.

Why Does it Matter?

Put simply, trauma is at the root of mental health issues. It lingers. And with a lack of support, it can become unmanageable. Many people struggle with trauma, and it can have a massive impact on their mental health and well-being.

It matters because people are dying at unprecedented rates. Suicide is the 11th leading cause of death in the United States (Suicide Statistics, 2024). Within that statistic, veterans are one of the most cited groups to be susceptible to trauma and twice as likely to succumb to suicide. Lack of treatment is killing people.

If you can't healthily process your trauma, it shows up somewhere else, plaguing your mental and/or physical health. Unfortunately, there's no quick or simple fix because everyone reacts to distress differently. But discovering how to cope healthily is one of the most valuable skills you can learn.

Common Examples of Traumatic Events

No one is immune to trauma. Living in our world is traumatic, almost by definition. Here are some common ways humans experience trauma, simply by existing in the here and now.

Current World Events

I was a sophomore in high school when 9/11 happened. A national traumatic event. Even though I was living in Maryland, I had family living in Manhattan, close to where the World Trade Center was. I was immediately worried about them, and back then, we did not have cell phones, so there was no way to immediately contact someone. Thankfully, my aunt and uncle were safe. I consider myself lucky, as many others were not and lost loved ones that day. The closer you are to a large-scale traumatic event like this, the longer it will affect you. While traumas were more isolated in past centuries, as information simply wasn't accessible, in the modern world, we experience events collectively in an entirely new way. Think about just the past few years: A major global recession, a pandemic, and Black Lives Matter protests, all in short succession. In recent years, active shootings have become more prevalent, with there being 118 active shooter incidents since 1999 (Vigderman & Turner, 2024).

Any Kind of Grief or Loss

Death of a family member or friend, a relationship, a pet—any person, place, or even thing you've developed an attachment with. Even the most experienced practitioners of non-attachment will get upset about losing their dog. Grief is universally traumatic, and everyone processes it differently. My first experience with losing a family member was when my maternal grandfather passed when I was 16 years old. That was incredibly traumatic for me because he was one of the few male figures in my life whom I actually felt safe around. His death, as well as my maternal grandmother's (she passed 10 years after he did), are the hardest ones that still hit me as if they happened yesterday.

Adverse Childhood Experiences (ACEs)

According to the U.S. Centers for Disease Control and Prevention (CDC, 2024), nearly 64% of adults report having at least one adverse childhood experience (ACE), while approximately 17% of people will experience at least four *(raises hand)*. These experiences can include violence, abuse, or neglect, encompassing aspects of a child's environment that undermine their sense of safety, stability, and ability to form healthy bonds with others. Households with substance use problems, mental health issues, instability due to parental separation, or instability due to household members being in jail or prison are just a handful of the adverse experiences children may go through. Traumatic experiences that impact health and well-being long-term also include food insecurity, temporary or sustained homelessness, or discrimination. All of these experiences can morph into different types of mental health issues later in life.

Severe Mental Health

You may be familiar with common mental health issues such as anxiety disorders, depression, PTSD, bipolar disorder, schizophrenia, and various personality disorders. As practitioners, one of our primary roles during an initial intake assessment is to ask about past experiences of abuse and neglect, especially if those experiences have not been previously disclosed. Social workers, in particular, are mandated reporters in these situations. When a client shares such experiences, it becomes an area we will revisit when they feel ready.

With clients, I often wonder if what they've shared could be tied to trauma. It's not uncommon for past experiences, such as trauma, grief, or loss, to be revealed over time. Sometimes, clients may not be ready to discuss these events during the initial stages of therapy. Avoidance is a common response. While this can be challenging, as clients are there to work through their problems, everyone's comfort is at their own pace.

Post Traumatic Stress Disorder (PTSD) and C-PTSD

PTSD can show in many ways, including anxiety, depression, Attention Deficit Hyperactivity Disorder, bipolar disorder, self-esteem issues, and a wide range of other mental health challenges. At its core, PTSD is the inability to move past a traumatic event. Life may feel overwhelming, with flashbacks that replay the experience as though it's happening all over again. People might hear sounds or smell scents that remind them of the trauma—it's remarkable how deeply our senses are linked to memory. In some cases, the brain may try to protect itself by blocking specific memories of the trauma, yet it can still feel as if you're stuck in that moment. Triggers, such as loud noises, crowded places, or even the anniversary of the traumatic event, can make you feel like you are reliving a traumatic experience. Over time, reliving this trauma repeatedly contributes to the development of anxiety, depression, ADHD, and self-esteem struggles, among just about any other mental illness.

You are likely already familiar with PTSD in the context of the military. Soldiers going into war, prolonged separation from their families, and people dying around them at an alarming rate are all contributors to the suicide rates among veterans. Given the degree of suffering and trauma they face, it's tragic but understandable why the non-adjusted suicide rates for veterans are almost twice as high as for non-veterans (Suicide Statistics, 2024). The mental anguish endured grants a need for far better support for veterans and, generally, anybody affected by the lasting impacts of trauma. I have such a profound respect for the military, especially because so many of my neighbors are veterans or are still in active service. A lot of them are also African American, which makes me respect them even more because they have fought for a country where systemic racism is so prevalent. They are better and stronger people than I am.

PTSD in Everyday Life

Complex Post Traumatic Stress Disorder (C-PTSD) is continued and prolonged exposure to traumatic events from which there is no escape. It is a spectrum that most of us can relate to, at least in some way. As a child, you are completely vulnerable to whatever situation you are born into.

Being raised by an alcoholic parent with a traumatic history, I understand how complicated and tangled reflecting on past horrific experiences can be. Prolonged and repetitive exposure to a series of traumatic events, which, again, whether big or small, accumulate into long-term effects.

My childhood, raised by a rage-fueled alcoholic father, was a period of prolonged exposure to him, his disease, and the trauma of a sustained, chaotic, and unsafe living situation. It's likely the reason for my Crohn's disease. Generational cycles are, unfortunately, typical. My alcoholic parent had their own traumatic history that wasn't dealt with healthily. In a way, I was being traumatized by their trauma through their actions.

Discrimination is another, unfortunately, common traumatic experience that many people fairly easily understand. As you can imagine, or perhaps have experienced personally, many minorities face discrimination that, over time, evolves into trauma. In my practice, I have heard experiences of clients enduring racial comments

and having to "just get over it" to keep their employment. One of my clients, a Black woman teaching in a predominantly white school, endured racist comments and behavior so often that it eventually led to her seeking therapy, where I found her in my inbox.

Another way trauma pops up in our mental health is through something called adjustment disorder. This disorder is another maladaptive response to outside stressors and, although typically not as long-lasting as PTSD and C-PTSD, combines similar symptoms that play out milder and less severe in comparison.

At any level of severity, daily symptoms like these can be incapacitating, and I've found a deep mind-body-spirit connection to be completely essential in coping with it.

The Modern-Day Trinity: Mind-Body-Spirit Connection

Intro to Mind-Body-Spirit Connection

I have found that the way we perceive life, others, and our relationships is deeply connected to a triad of tenets of our well-being:

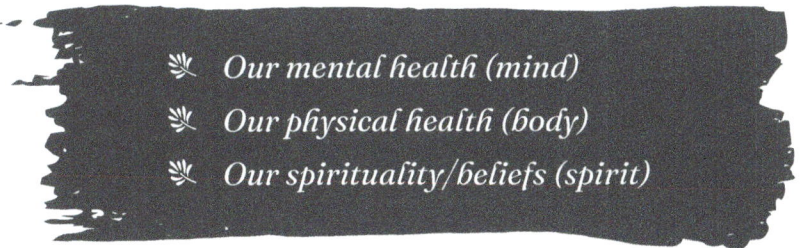

Our mental health (mind)
Our physical health (body)
Our spirituality/beliefs (spirit)

Mental health shapes how we view the world, our reactions to life's challenges, the emotional impact of those experiences, and the invisible struggles others may not see but are just as real. It's essential to recognize these impacts and understand that every part of our being—body, mind, and spirit—can experience illness or imbalance.

Consider this: why is catching a cold often seen as something so trivial, but having a depressive episode or an anxiety attack can feel like a big deal?

The Mind

There's no way to test for mental health like you can for the flu...yet. Mental health is complex, tricky, and often challenging to diagnose. Asking for help can be just as difficult. You might hear phrases like, "What do you mean you're depressed? Why are you anxious?" or "You seem like you have it all together...good job, nice house, living the dream...what's the issue?" My father literally said this to my aunt/his sister. The girl who lost the same mother he did. (Can you imagine?)

Let me clarify, first and upfront: this is all simply gaslighting, dismissing the very real struggles that so many of us face, including myself.

When it comes to mental health, there's often an automatic assumption that something is "wrong" with you. Struggling with something doesn't make you a bad person. There's no shame in it; it doesn't make you broken; it makes you REAL. It makes you human, and as a human, you deserve to support and care for your internal trinity of mind, body, and spirit.

Maintaining a healthy mindset is essential not just for your own well-being but for the good of your relationships. Your family, friends, loved ones, and even your pets are impacted by your mental wellness. How you interact with others is important; sometimes, often, those interactions reflect unresolved issues you may have yet to fully deal with. Unresolved trauma can show up in relationships in many ways, making the experience difficult for both you and the other person.

The Body

When we talk about the body, we're referring to our physical health—the very body we walk around in every day! You only get one body in this lifetime. It's essential to cherish it so it can carry you through life. And while physical health is important, an added benefit to balance within the body is mental well-being.

There's also a chemical component to this connection. Changes in the body can stimulate endorphins, reduce cortisol, and release dopamine. These chemicals directly affect how we feel physically and mentally. Chemical imbalances in the brain play a significant role in conditions like depression. Endorphins—the brain chemical that makes you happy—are particularly adept at bringing us closer to our spirit. Our body is, in fact, a reflection of our nature, and despite what some may believe, evidence points in the direction that nature and nurture work *together* in shaping who we are.

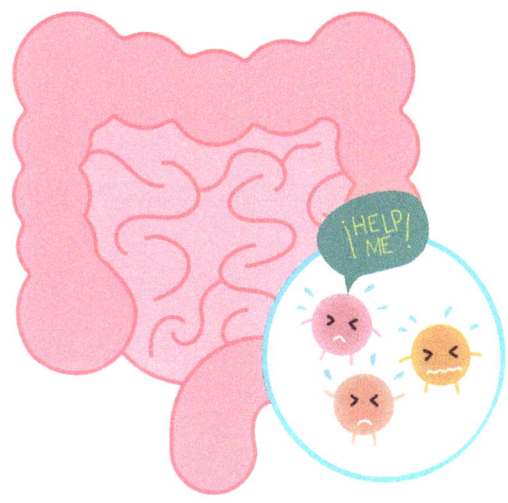

The Spirit

In European—and euro-colonized areas, the relationship between body and spirit is often seen as separate, but in other cultures around the world, body and spirit have long been understood to be deeply interconnected. Your spirit is your soul, as well as the part of you that connects to a higher power and the energy of loved ones who have passed. It's less about specifics and more about feelings of warmth, connection, support, and love. Spirit is your connection to the universe as a whole, to the planet, and even to the energetic ties between all things, beings, and people.

Religion and spirituality are deeply personal, and can therefore be sensitive subjects, and often, so often we prefer to avoid this discomfort. But balance is key.

For purposes of this book, we'll define Spirit as the feeling of being connected to the universe. Having a belief in a higher power, however you define that. Spirit is what connects us all, not just to each other, but to something greater. Spirit is what bridges the mind and body.

When you feel disconnected from this higher power, you can lose yourself and your sense of connection to others. It's a domino effect. You become anchorless. Adrift. Without this, you may lose sight of your goals, values, beliefs, and even those you admire. Without clarity in your spirit, it's like a table missing a leg. It just doesn't stand right.

Take five minutes to write unfiltered thoughts without judgment on the topic of "How I define Spirit."

....
....
....
....
....
....
....
....
....
....
....
....
....
....
....
....
....
....

Spirituality:
How it impacts the Mind/
Body Connection

My History and Spirituality

I grew up in the Catholic Church. I took my First Communion and went through Confirmation. I took the full route and checked all the boxes: Attending Sunday school and church regularly to prepare for religious ceremonies. I continued this lifestyle full-time until I was 24, and my parents even paid for me to get married in the church. While I did and do love my husband, I can also see, in retrospect, my marriage as a way of trying to escape my father's control.

Being that I grew up in the Catholic church, I was forced to bury my secret truth deep within me. I completely lucked out that the person I chose to marry was my best friend. We have a great partnership, and he accepts me, all my trauma, as well as my bisexuality. We've made our path and our roles together. My husband grew up Catholic as well, but we've disengaged from Catholicism together, which I'm grateful for, as we get to raise our daughter with an open mind and, hopefully, free of judgment. Seeing my child's pride flag hung up openly in her room heals something deep within me.

I attended Salisbury University on Maryland's Eastern Shore, about two and a half hours from where I grew up. Though it was in-state, it felt far enough that I could break free from my dad's control. My mother found a Catholic church near campus, and I remember attending a few services, but each time, I felt detached, thinking I wouldn't get anything out of it. My newfound sense of freedom meant I only went to church on holidays while home from college. I felt so guilty about that. Guilt and confusion consumed me, but deep down, I knew I still believed in some sort of higher power.

MINDFULNESS BRINGS CLARITY

It eventually became clear to me that it was the rules of Catholicism that plagued my mind. I had always questioned some of the church's teachings. Even as a five or six-year-old, I couldn't understand why women couldn't be priests. I scrutinized these issues more as I got older, but some aspects were so deeply ingrained in me that they felt almost invisible. It seemed like homosexuality and other taboo topics were not just condemned but erased, avoided altogether.

One of my first crushes was a girl neighbor. I remember us kissing, and at one point, I remember feeling I was going to be punished or deeply judged. I didn't want my higher power to protect me. I wanted him not to judge me. Even things like getting a divorce were also looked down upon. I give a lot of credit to my mom and other women who can return to church and still feel accepted. Even now, I sometimes think I offend her and folks on both sides of my family, but honestly, I think it's awesome that the church works for them. I'm so glad that people can feel great when they go. While it doesn't do for me what it does for them, I've found other things that feel more fulfilling spiritually.

In my junior year of college, halfway into my psychology program, my friend's mother showed us *The Secret*, a documentary-style movie about the law of attraction and mindset (Byrne, 2006). It was incredibly eye-opening. The law of attraction states that positive thoughts and actions lead to positive outcomes. The flip side is equally true, as negative attracts negative. Our thoughts have energy, as well as the power to enact little changes that can, in turn, enact big changes and positive outcomes. I applied this personally, and I remember the movie made it feel like there were no rules. It felt so freeing. I began to feel I could have a say and exert control over things, yet there was still a way to connect to a higher power. There were more spiritual parts and religious aspects that I could draw from that spoke to me. It just felt right. Since then, I've customized my mind-body-spirit trinity, especially my spirit. I started to take the parts of religion that resonated, alongside my psychology studies and personal mental health, which I'm passionate about, including a few Eastern influences along the way.

There are aspects of religion that still work for this mind-body-spirit trinity, such as my lifelong desire for prayer. Praying reminds me of meditation. The idea of praying to God, the universe, or any higher power is all the same. We throw out our thoughts to something we believe in that is bigger than ourselves.

Learning more about meditation and other similar practices in grad school was life-changing for me because I felt good connecting and communicating with my higher power from the comfort of my home, and not having to be in a church.

A big part of the spirit is energy. I'm talking about the kind of energy where you feel connected to a higher power; sometimes you feel like listening, praying, or meditating, and sometimes you just feel like talking/praying. My Buddhas, candles, incense, and crystals are all things that help me bring my positive energy.

With Cognitive Behavioral Therapy (CBT), typically, you're working with a therapist to change your negative thinking. With the help of meditation, prayer, and connecting with a higher power, I felt I could do some of these CBT techniques myself, which empowered me to believe I could heal myself on my terms. CBT and all of these interventions and modalities are super helpful. If our brains are trained a certain way, we need to retrain our brains. And that takes time, patience, and a lot of quiet to think and observe your thoughts. My friends and I formed an unofficial "Healing Group of Four." Together, we've been instrumental in building new foundations.

Unpacking religious trauma takes time and the right path. If people have experienced trauma within the religious setting, they probably would not feel comfortable incorporating anything from that until they worked through that and reintegrated from that experience or situation. Anyone feeling anti-spiritual or anti-religious likely has some religious trauma. I can't stress enough how pivotal it is to work with someone specialized in this. Luckily, there are plenty of qualified people out there who can help you walk through these complex problems.

There is a strong intersectionality between Catholicism, Buddhism, Spirituality, and psychology. When I say *psychology*, I'm not talking about the "good vibes only" of pop psychology but rather being genuinely introspective. I took a course, PSYC 305: Positive Psychology, that introduced me to concepts I'd never considered before. I learned what positive affirmations were, which helped me start to be kind to myself without feeling unauthentic or cheesy. I slowly began saying positive things about myself and others. Writing down the affirmations multiple times, on the mirror, on a post-it note, or anywhere I could see, over time, helped to retrain my brain. It is not an easy process. You have to be diligent.

Sometimes, jumping from negative to positive thoughts feels impossible and fake. That's why starting with neutral statements can be an easy introduction to reshaping your thinking. A neutral statement might sound like: "I have legs that allow me to walk down the street to my job." This isn't a positive or negative statement but simply a neutral fact. By acknowledging these neutral facts, the mind can begin to weed out negativity without the pressure of forcing positivity. It's a process. Sometimes, you've got to "fake it 'til you make it," and that's okay. It's important to give yourself grace if it doesn't feel entirely authentic at first. If you stick with it long enough, the authenticity will come.

The power of positive thinking and the law of attraction involve more than just wishful thinking; they require visualizing where you want to be. In 2017, when my husband and I were looking for our "dream home," we had a clear vision of what we wanted. After a few months, he found a neighborhood we hadn't yet explored, and it turned out to have exactly the type of home we were looking for. The lot was perfect, nestled against the woods, and the neighbors turned out to be just as wonderful as we'd hoped. It felt like it was truly meant to be.

In September 2022, we manifested our dream car. Despite Toyota telling us, "We're not sure which RAV4 you'll get; it's just whatever comes off the truck," we ended up with exactly the one we wanted. That experience reaffirmed my belief in the power of manifestation. And while I'm not *positive* it's possible to manifest a healthy child, it certainly feels like we did. All we focused on was wanting a healthy baby, one who would be loved and supported for who they are. We were fortunate in how things unfolded during the pregnancy of our daughter, who turned ten in January 2025.

But we're not special. You can manifest experiences as well. A close friend of mine (and my aforementioned yoga buddy) also manifested something she had been dreaming about for years: tickets to a Taylor Swift concert. To her surprise, her boss paid for the tickets as a gift, and it came completely out of the blue. She wasn't expecting it at all, but she had always felt joy when someone she knew was able to attend one of Taylor's concerts, knowing that someday, it would be her turn.

Self-Help Gurus Over the Years

For quite some time now, I've been following affirmations from self-help gurus, with Mike Dooley being one of my favorites. He encourages people to stop worrying about the "how" and break free from the hamster wheel of worrying. It can be incredibly difficult to escape that spiral of worry. When I started reading his work, I realized I didn't need to focus on the details of "how" things would happen, but instead on the result and what I truly wanted.

The creation of Clarity Wellness Solutions is a perfect example of this shift in mindset. I remember telling people as young as middle school that I was going to have a mental health practice. But at the time, it was hard for me to truly visualize it. It felt almost out of reach, but I held onto the goal. Now, as I write this book, we are four years into running a successful telehealth practice.

Eckhart Tolle—another major inspiration for me. During spring break in college, a few friends and I began reading his work, which immediately resonated with me. His writing speaks deeply about our inherent goodness and how therapy can help uncover and express that goodness. Spirituality, as he describes it, is not about rigid beliefs or the identity you build around them. It's about your mindset.

Holding onto fixed beliefs can create a barrier to deeper spiritual awareness, something I've observed in many "religious" individuals who seem stuck at a surface level. I came to realize that true spiritual awareness shapes how we act and how we interact with others.

One of the key ideas Eckhart Tolle introduced me to is a more profound understanding of the ego and its role in our consciousness. While I had a basic understanding of Freud's theory of the ego from my psychology background, Eckhart's explanation resonated much deeper (Freud, 1962). Letting go of the ego allows us to connect more fully with our spirit or higher power because the ego often creates inner resistance, negativity, and judgment—aka what hinders true connection.

Tolle also elaborates on the idea of the pain body as a result of unprocessed trauma. Since trauma lives in the fascia of the muscles, it is physically present in us, often causing pain in our bodies. Eckhart simply calls this the "pain body" (Tolle, 2005). A happy, positive thought is indigestible to the pain body. It can only feed on negative thoughts because only those thoughts are compatible with its energy field.

I cannot speak of my inspirations throughout this journey without mentioning Brené Brown. *The Gifts of Imperfection* was one of my favorite and first books from Brené (Brown, 2010). It showed me the tools for wholehearted living and doubling down on the messages from the Spirit already on my path. She has resonated so much with me around shame and guilt. All of her shame research resonates greatly with people and resonated with me.

How Spirituality Affects Mental Health

Spirituality has had a significant effect on my mental health. I always felt immense pressure from my family to have my spiritual beliefs be a certain way, so it never felt like my spirituality was my choice. I also felt rejected for my sexuality, which made me feel like an outsider in religion anyway. There was a positive side, too, though. When I finally found my trinity of what works for me as a higher power, I felt like I had finally found something I could rely on. I felt supported in my positive thinking, which gave me the desire to start praying and meditating.

Over time, this helped my self-esteem and made me feel better about myself. It became clear that I was not so broken after all. My crippling anxiety became manageable, and I saw a way out. I noticed that I could achieve this dream of having my therapy practice on my own—and, in fact, I already DID. I finally found a way to help myself that I hadn't found before, that I had not yet learned at that point in my life, and I am grateful to say I can now help others.

Define your own Mind-Body-Spirit Connection

....

....

....

....

....

....

....

....

....

....

....

....

....

....

....

....

....

....

....

My Family History of Mental Health

Mental health is such a big part of my family history. My mom is a nurse, and I grew up very physically health-oriented. I come from an "if your head hurts, take this" sort of family. You may think that the healthcare profession would be more aware of *mental* health, but my mother neglected those aspects despite being a nurse for her whole career.

I remember being in my teens and learning that my paternal grandmother passed from suicide when my father was a young child. Severe mental illness ran in our genes and has been a part of our family history. Suicide is a mental health/mental illness-related action with devastating consequences, and our healthcare system failed her if, indeed, that is how she died. I was always interested in pursuing psychology, even before I learned that's how my grandmother passed. I know now that's why I was strongly called to this field. I can only imagine the trauma my family endured and sometimes wonder if I am righting a wrong. I feel like my family tried to erase her and her memory because of how she died, and it feels like I am protecting my legacy. I want to make things better for my daughter and future generations, to not be so judged, despite whatever you might be dealing with mentally.

Coping, Medication, Mental Health, and Mind-Body Connection Methods

There is no shame in needing medication. I am on medication myself, and I am not ashamed of it, but it is important to remember that it isn't the only way to solve things. Some illnesses are more likely to need to be medicated, but there are plenty of options to consider first. The first step before anything is to recognize what your problem is.

Oftentimes, some needs are more immediate, and those issues must be addressed first. That is something I have seen and helped patients work through in my clinic. Problems like addiction and alcoholism are rooted deep and have underlying trauma to work through. Consider your own coping skills for trauma. Are they healthy?

As kids, we only know what we are taught by family or school. Whether healthy or not, we typically develop the coping skills of our caregivers. It is usually not so black and white from what I have seen, but you either move toward the same coping skills you've observed in your caregivers, or you move completely away from them. Common examples of some negative coping habits are the overuse of alcohol and other drugs, sex, and gambling, but can include anything that helps you disassociate or makes your life unmanageable.

These things are usually okay in balance, but when utilized as a coping strategy, without moderation, they are quite dangerous. If these habits help you to block out, not relive—and heal from—your trauma, it will always feel better than not, no matter what may be sacrificed in the meantime. That's why addiction is a disease. These "strategies" become so dependent on one's well-being that they affect daily routine, relationships, and everything in between.

When you become dependent on these vices, you choose the negative coping habit over other things in your life. Addiction may start as a coping mechanism, but eventually, it doesn't feel like a choice anymore. If you're still in the hamster wheel and no one pulls you out, it becomes so ingrained that it takes over you. Then, when you lose control, you have to stop doing whatever it is that you're doing to cope.

Of course, as with everything, there's a spectrum with different severities. There are inpatient programs for addiction if you know you're far on that spectrum. If you have greater support needs, those resources are out there. If it does ever get that bad for you, there is a way out there to get that help, and having support is crucial for working through addiction. AA and Al-Anon are just two examples of many different types of support groups that help folks heal from negative coping habits. We are fortunate to have progressed into a period where there is a support group for anything. Especially with virtual options available, there are many different communities out there and ways for people to connect. This is what I mean when I constantly say "you are not alone."

Having a community of people who understands you provides a level of comfort and empathy that is hard to find elsewhere. Something about feeling alone breeds intrusive thoughts, even for the most independent. We usually can't do it on our own, and that's okay. It doesn't mean there isn't a way out. You're not broken, but it's easy to stay in that mindset without support.

Leaning on whomever it might be to get you out of an emotional spiral is important when you are struggling. Support groups, in person or virtually, are helpful because someone is always going through the same thing. Whether it's a person or group, you need to have someone you can lean on during a crisis or thoughts of self-harm or suicide. Our lowest moments can be scary, and it's wild what the brain can think and make you want to do.

I can say firsthand that addiction does not "look a certain way." My dad was very functional in his alcoholism for so much of his life. Growing up, my dad always used alcohol as a way to cope after work. We were always taken care of, and I am grateful for that. He woke up, made sure we went to school, always had a good job, and financially provided for my family. Somewhere in between, when he wasn't working, golf became his big thing on the weekends, and he would drink a whole lot there.

While he worked very hard, he didn't spend a lot of time with us. Mom worked the night shift, and every day, she'd be sleeping when

we got home from school, and we would have about 20 minutes with Dad before bedtime. Mom was off on the weekends, and with my sister, it just felt like the three of us. Dad would always be golfing. We'd go to church Saturday night, and going out to dinner was the most family time we would have outside of an occasional vacation. I'd go to friends' houses and see their dads were home on weekends, and I always thought it was so strange. My mom would describe their relationship as two ships passing in the night, but realistically, we were four ships passing in the night, living our lives, sometimes co-existing.

REFERENCE RESOURCES

Shattering the Stigma of Medication

Medication is a terrifying possibility for many people. A lot of parents I speak with express concern for their children turning into zombies or other extreme fears that are simply not going to take place. I often think about a brace metaphor when explaining how medication works. If you're dealing with some sort of injury to your knee, you would wear a brace, right? To maybe make it a little bit easier or less painful to walk? Well, think of the medication as that brace. It's just trying to make life easier and a little bit less painful.

Medication will not necessarily cure or heal your problems. It is just a brace. It can make it easier to get through your day, helping you focus or calm racing thoughts. The right medication will not completely change you, but rather make you more effective in whatever the goal might be.

Somatic healing methods are a great option if medication is not your thing. These methods release the traumatic energy that gets trapped in the body. There are different ways to release this. Breathwork, for instance, uses controlled breathing to calm the nervous system, with different techniques offering benefits for restoring balance to the body. Movement exercises, such as gentle stretches, help release physical tension. Practices like yoga and Qi Gong combine light exercise with mindfulness, promoting overall body awareness.

For those seeking a more passive approach, visual techniques can be incredibly powerful. Guided imagery encourages visualization to help the mind and body work in harmony. In some cases, therapeutic touch methods provide a sense of safety and grounding. Craniosacral therapy (CST) and Reiki are alternative therapies that focus on healing through the body, CST through touch, and Reiki through energy. Massages and acupuncture are also common ways to release built-up trauma stored in the body that you may already be familiar with. All of these techniques are strong alternatives or excellent alongside traditional medication.

We all experience trauma. It is nearly impossible to escape trauma completely in your lifetime. Unfortunately, I come from a time when trauma and how that affects your mental health just wasn't discussed growing up. Trauma affects us in so many different ways, and you can't just ignore it like the Catholic Church wants to ignore the gays. Sorry, you can't. We're here. We exist.

We can't ignore trauma. Trauma is here, and ignoring it is not going to make it go away; it's just going to get worse. I want us to accept our traumas. Whatever they are, however big or small they are, they matter. It is worth it to put down all of the traumas you're still carrying. You are worthy of healing.

ROOT CHAKRA

In yogic and spiritual traditions, chakras are considered energy centers within the body, visualized as spinning wheels or discs, that are believed to influence physical, mental, emotional, and spiritual well-being.

Base/Root Chakra - Yoga Squat/Garland Pose

The root chakra is located at the base of the spine and is associated with grounding, security, and survival. If you were emotionally neglected at any point during your childhood, your sense of security and safety might have been compromised, thus blocking your root chakra. Use this pose to clear any blockages from this area.

How does Trauma Come Into Play?

To understand how trauma comes into play in our lives, we need to understand what trauma is. Knowledge is power, as they say. If we know what it is, we can understand how it might manifest. Trauma is a spectrum of experiences. In short, trauma is any adverse event that took place in our lives that our body is incapable of making sense of.

Trauma gets stuck in our bodies. Have you ever heard about trauma being stored in the hips? There's truth to that. Often, when people think of "trauma," they think of something major—life-altering injuries, deaths, extreme violence. There are also more minor traumas we experience throughout life, which accumulate in our bodies if not properly integrated.

Here's a common event many might not first recognize as trauma. The first day of school. This day used to be very traumatic for me. I got lost a lot. I was late a lot. Because I was late a lot, it developed into terrible anxiety anytime I was running late. My heart would be racing, and I would be sweating. I was so worried I would get in trouble. In 8th grade, I got reprimanded by my math teacher for

being a few minutes late (it was the first day! She couldn't give me a break?). I came home and cried to my mom when she woke up from her nap. In her tired haze, she just said, "I'm sorry, sweetie". It felt like I was never going to be free of this anxious feeling.

I feel like the first day always went the same way for me. I remember thinking, "It's the first day of school. What is going to happen this time?" I would wake up crying to my mom about having to go to school. The first day was so traumatic for me. It carried on through my life. Something that most people wouldn't consider very traumatic, something almost small and insignificant to most others, was something that affected new things for me, even after I graduated and no longer had a "first day of school." Anything I was new to, I felt those same first-day jitters. I still wondered what might happen.

Trauma comes in all forms. Did you ever have to move away? Did you ever have to watch a friend move away? These can be types of trauma. Did you move around a lot as a kid? That can be another form of trauma.

My "military brat" clients talk about this a lot. They talk about never having a stable place to stay or a place to call home. Having to move around a lot as a kid can be very traumatic, and it is also often overlooked, as it's, well, common. Whether it's the child leaving or whether it's just one of the parents leaving, that's hard. When the entire family moves, the child loses friends, teachers, and peers. That feeling of starting over can have a huge impact on mental health.

There are also the more extreme trauma examples, the ones people always think of. Sexual assault (SA), domestic violence (DV), child abuse, suicide, and witnessing death. There are many more. These are some of the traumas that show up the most obviously in relationships, as well as our ability to feel safe in our bodies.

Trauma can especially show up in romantic relationships. You might not know that you don't feel safe in your body until you are with someone else. Relationships tend to highlight things we didn't notice at first. The deeper our connection grows with another person, the more our traumas seem to come to a head.

These traumas also come back to haunt us when we become parents. Things hit us differently when we are raising kids of our own. We're doing it for a few years, and then suddenly realize, "Why wasn't it like this for me?" We start to recall what it was like when we were one, two, three…and further on. We're suddenly reminded of the things we went through in the dynamics of our parent-child relationships.

It's a different perspective, but it also makes us realize there are certain things that we wouldn't necessarily put our child through. There's something about those memories that come back to haunt us. We might be doing it for a few years and doing our best, and we start to question: "Why wasn't my childhood like this for me?"

We gain a new perspective. On the one hand, we now know what it might have been like for our parents to raise children. We might have been angry about some of the things that our parents did or said to us, but now that we are grown up, we've gained a new understanding of it. Alternatively, we might realize that we could never do some of the things to our own children.

For example, I can apologize to my daughter if I accidentally raise my voice, something I never experienced growing up. I am also thankful that I have been able to walk away from my daughter before "spanking" her. I did it one time when she was two or three years old, and was horrified immediately, and have not done it since. I'm much more aware of my emotional regulation than my father was. I'm thankful I have broken that cycle in that way.

The Mind-Body Connection

As mentioned, little and big traumas can and do occur throughout our lifetimes. Unfortunately, those traumas and the effects they have on our bodies don't just disappear. They stay with us. Literally.

There is a thin covering over our muscles called the fascia; this is where our traumas are stored.

Eckart Tolle described the trauma as the "pain body." It is essentially a physical, emotional, or mental pain that gets trapped in our bodies. A lot of these traumas can manifest as physical pain in the body, thus the pain body.

When I first read his book, *A New Earth*, I wasn't even aware of my own pain body (aka trauma). I read it for the first time as a senior in college and was so unaware of my pain body at the time that I'm rereading it now to help me identify my trauma. Reading it from this perspective brings a new type of healing for me (Tolle, 2025).

My dad's been coming to mind a lot recently. The first time I read the book, I thought a lot about him, so it makes sense that I am thinking about him again. Though I am thinking more about my dad and his mother, my grandmother. I think about the pain bodies that they didn't deal with, and how that affected me. My grandmother's depression was treated a lot with physical remedies, medications to treat physical ailments like epilepsy, with her childhood trauma going completely unaddressed. Her trauma affected her physically and led to her taking her own life.

That's the thing. If we don't deal with our pain bodies, they can get passed down through generations. Have you ever heard the term "generational trauma"? Or how about the phrase "sins of the father"? There's a long explanation to it and lots of research to dig through, but the short version is: Generational trauma is when pain bodies go unaddressed over and over and over again, and the traumas keep adding up and affecting different people, in different generations, the same way. Which is why I referred to it as a "cycle"; it keeps repeating until we put a stop to it. That is something we need to work on.

Triggers

Pain bodies also relate to triggers. Someone in childhood who was neglected or abandoned by one or both parents has experienced pretty major trauma. That person will develop a pain body that becomes triggered in any situation that reminds them even slightly of the pain of abandonment.

If we are present in our physical bodies when the pain body pops its head up—aka, we are not disassociating but truly engaged in the situation at hand—part of that traumatic response is to burn up some of the negative emotional energy and turn it into what Tolle calls, capital P, Presence. The rest of the pain body will withdraw and wait for a time when we are less present to pop back up (Tolle, 2005).

How long might these pain bodies last? It depends on the density of an individual's pain body and the degree or intensity of the individual's arising Presence. But a more important question might be, "How long does it take to become free of identification with the pain body?"

See, it's not necessarily the pain body that causes suffering, but our identification with it. That identification causes us to inflict pain on ourselves and others. It is the identification of the pain body that forces us to relive the past again and again. It is the identification of the pain body that keeps us in a state of unconsciousness.

Back to the question: How long does it take to become free of identification with the pain body? The answer? No time at all. If we are aware of the pain body and how it manifests, we can break our identification with it. When the pain body is activated, remind yourself that the feeling is the pain body within you and not your identity. It doesn't define who you are.

There is an amazing book, *The Body Keeps the Score*, that talks about how the body remembers the traumas it's lived through and then manifests that (van der Kolk, 2015). The body can even manifest that trauma physically.

Mental health meets physical health in different ways. Sometimes trauma might manifest as a headache or neckache, where we assume that we slept wrong. Sometimes, it might be a stomachache. In reality, it might be an outward symptom of trauma and stress. Of course, not every ache and pain is trauma manifesting itself, but if you've been feeling particularly stressed or triggered, it might be time to do some self-reflection.

Recently, I was getting a massage, and my masseuse noticed how extra tense my shoulders were. Could it be that I've been hunched over my computer? I'm always on my computer, though, so it shouldn't be anything new. I told her I'd had an especially stressful week at work. My shoulders weren't more tense than usual because I was hunched over my computer. My shoulders were more tense because of the stressors.

By being mindful of our mental states, we can consider what stressors might be popping up in our lives, which also helps us become aware of how those stressors affect us.

One of my clients had been diagnosed with pseudotumor cerebri syndrome, which is a condition that causes pressure to increase in our skull for no apparent reason. I had never heard of this until she told me about it, but the brain thinks it has a brain tumor. It presents the same symptoms. From pressure headaches to blurry vision, all kinds of symptoms appear. She worked on treating this for a year, and thankfully, now she's okay. Her diagnosis coincided with a very traumatic car accident—another example of how mental stress can cause physical symptoms.

I have another client who had something similar. Kristy suffered from childhood abuse and neglect. In her adulthood, she endures chronic migraines for no apparent reason. Could the migraines be caused by that trauma from her childhood? I think so.

Systemic and Generational Trauma

What is systemic trauma? This is trauma that affects a large group of collective individuals. Black Americans, Holocaust survivors, and Indigenous communities are just a few examples that can and have been affected by systemic trauma. Millions of people are continuously faced with the trauma of the system. Katherine Milligan, Laura Calderon de la Barca, and John Kania point out in their Collective Change Lab article "Guiding questions to identify systemic trauma" that systemic trauma is especially prevalent in communities that have experienced colonization or other large-scale events (Milligan et al., 2024).

Other institutions and systems also contribute to systemic trauma. Schools, religious institutions, the military, workplace settings, hospitals, and the prison industrial complex are examples of environments that might add to this type of trauma (Goldsmith et al., 2014). Additionally, agencies such as the police, the foster care system, immigration, federal assistance, disaster management, and the media can have an effect. Finally, conflicts such as war, terrorism, and refugees, and the dynamics of racism, sexism, discrimination, bullying, and homophobia are all things that contribute to systemic trauma.

One of my previous clients, an African American, once shared, "I'm only a couple of generations away from slavery." For reference, the last enslaved group of Americans was freed on June 19, 1865, roughly 160 years ago, and if people lived until about 80, which they occasionally did at that point in history, it is possible that the last person who was enslaved could have lived until the mid-1900s! Which gives only two or three generations of distance from slavery.

That is what systemic trauma is and what it does. My client is still affected by slavery. Daily. In her own body. Systemic trauma stays with you. We can't—or often just don't—address things like that. We need to acknowledge things like this to heal from them.

Consider now the combination of systemic and generational trauma existing inside my client's body.

How does generational trauma differ from systemic trauma? Generational trauma is the passing down of traumas and psychological or emotional wounds from one generation to the next. Part of it comes from our genes, but part of it also comes from how we are raised. Nature and nurture combine in a complex, tangled web.

If I were raised by someone who was traumatized by some event in their youth that they never dealt with, that trauma would affect me as well. It's always lingering in our blood and body, and it shows up in the energy from that caregiver.

Another example of generational trauma comes from passing down negative or positive coping skills. "Don't trust anyone. That's how you survive. Life is dark, and people aren't trustworthy." That is an unfortunately common example. If parents don't feel safe in the world, they are likely to teach their kids the same thing. Parents often think, "Whatever I do to cope, that's how you're going to cope." So many of my clients have described their parents teaching them in this way, and they all have one thing in common: anxiety in adulthood.

As children, we often feel trapped in our circumstances. It's only as adults that we start to confront our trauma and realize that our thought processes may not be helpful. We can discover healthier ways to live and heal. We don't have to stay isolated; a supportive community can remind us that we're not alone. To overcome our struggles, we must face them directly and break the cycle of generational trauma. Just because a pattern is familiar doesn't mean it's good for us; we need to change what doesn't serve us.

I have a grandmother who died from suicide in 1968, which is still affecting my family today. My father never got any therapy or other way to cope with his mother's suicide. Because it was never addressed, that laid the groundwork for his addiction. He also developed multiple mood and personality disorders. His unresolved trauma caused him to be verbally, mentally, and psychologically abusive to me and my sister.

There is some evidence that suggests generational trauma can happen in the uterus. A fetus can be exposed to chemicals caused by the mother's stress, which can impact their future development (Gillespie, 2023). In recent years, I have taken time to learn more about my dad's mother. I'm positive that he was exposed to stressors while in the womb. Add on the fact that she died when he was only six years old, and it's no wonder that he had so much trauma. I found out a few disturbing things while pregnant with my daughter. I'm sure some of my stress from that carried into her in utero. It is something that I might have to watch out for in the future.

Understand that we all have trauma. There is no one who hasn't experienced some form of it. It is up to us, however, to find out what it is, how it might manifest in us, and how to overcome it. Only you can do this work for yourself. No trauma isn't worth healing from or at least acknowledging in some way. We all deserve to live pain-free, stress-free lives.

We *can* get there by putting in the work. We must believe there is light on the other side of the tunnel. There is a way out. We just have to be willing to take the steps, one at a time, to make it to the other side. Don't be afraid to ask for help, either. It is there for you if you need it.

SACRAL CHAKRA POSE

Sacral Chakra - Bound Ankle Pose

The sacral chakra is located in the lower abdomen, and is associated with creativity, pleasure, and sexuality.

Chapter 3

Mindfulness

What is Mindfulness?

At its core, mindfulness is simply being aware of the present moment without judgment. It involves observing your thoughts, feelings, and surroundings with an open and accepting mindset. Every day, we are already mindful to a degree, but think about how often you take in the present moment to the point where you are putting in effort to truly understand it. True mindfulness requires intention and a dedicated effort.

Meditation is a well-known way to practice mindfulness, but there's a common misconception that mindfulness and meditation are the same. Many people think that if they're not "good" at meditation, mindfulness isn't for them. This couldn't be further from the truth. Mindfulness, like meditation, requires practice, and that's okay! It's about finding what works for you.

Personally, it was really hard for me to do that at first. Meditation and mindfulness are both like exercise; they take a consistent, habit-

forming type of practice. While meditation worked for me and many people across different cultures, it is certainly not the only mindfulness method.

Be careful not to equate feeling uncomfortable sitting still with your thoughts as being "bad" at meditation or mindfulness. Many of my clients with ADHD experience this initially, and if that's you, it's okay—it's valid, and it's normal to struggle. I work with clients to find a mindfulness practice that works for them, free of judgment. If stillness is difficult, there are plenty of other ways to practice mindfulness while staying active.

There are plenty of options for those who want to remain still but still need some movement. One of my clients with ADHD, for example, found mindfulness in fishing. While fishing doesn't require much physical movement, it offers a kind of movement in stillness. Plus, being in nature is an important aspect of healing as it is beneficial in reducing stress and supporting mental health. Anything you enjoy can be beneficial if it helps you step away from overstimulation and relax your mind, body, and spirit. Whether it's through fishing or another mindful activity, the key is to engage in something that brings you peace and realignment. It also helps to do anything with your hands. Anyone see that cult classic movie *Idle Hands*? I think the tagline was something like "idle hands are the devil's playpen" (Flender, 1999). Something to think about.

There is no right or wrong way to be present. The idea of being "good" or "not good" at mindfulness is a judgment that doesn't serve us in our practice. Mindfulness is varied and adaptable, with countless ways to utilize it. It has the power to heal both your brain and subconscious. You can be mindful while taking a shower, eating a meal, walking to work or school, or engaging in any task that might otherwise feel mundane. Anything can incorporate an element of being present in the here and now. As the cliche saying goes, everything in moderation. Mindfulness invites balance, allowing you to take control and keep things in harmony.

Defining Mindfulness vs. Meditation

Mindfulness is the practice of being fully present and aware of the moment without judgment. It's about observing your thoughts, feelings, and surroundings without trying to change or control them. You can practice mindfulness in any part of your day if you are simply aware and accept the present as it is.

Meditation, on the other hand, is an entirely separate practice. It's not the filtered image often portrayed in the media but rather the act of quieting the noise in your head. Meditation is about creating space to listen to your body, mind, and spirit. It's a time to slow down and connect with that inner trinity with intention. Meditation, much like prayer, allows you to open up to inner truths and messages that you may need to hear. It's a way to deepen your awareness and find clarity, helping you to connect with yourself on a deeper level.

As I mentioned in the previous chapter, I've been re-reading *A New Earth* by Eckhart Tolle. In this reading, Tolle discusses the concept of the ego and how deeply it can control us, often alongside the "pain body" (Tolle, 2005). The pain body, according to Tolle, as we've discussed, represents trauma stored physically in our bodies, manifesting as pain. Both the ego and the pain body thrive on negativity and judgment. Mindfulness can combat this, helping us achieve a state of nonjudgmental balance, fostering positivity and gratitude instead of feeding into the negativity.

Meditation is a strong technique in working toward mindfulness. It's a tool designed to heal the brain, providing a much-needed intervention for the mind. Think of it as the best brain therapy you can consume: an opportunity to reset, rebalance, and center away from the constant stream of negative thinking.

Types of Meditation

🌿 **Mindfulness (remain in the present)**

DEPRESSION RELEASE	STRESS RELIEF	ANXIETY

🌿 **Transcendental/Mantra (repeating mantras)**

INTUITION   MANTRA

🌿 **Spiritual meditation (connecting to a higher power)**

AWAKEN INTUITION   POSITIVITY

STRESS RELIEF
THROUGH NATURE

CONNECTING
WITH NATURE

43

❈ **Guided meditation, visualization, imagery**

INNER PEACE

DEPRESSION RELEASE

❈ **Loving-kindness meditation (toward self or someone else)**

LOVING KINDNESS

SELF-LOVE

❈ **Walking/movement meditation**

WALKING MOVEMENT

❈ **Body scan/progressive relaxation**

BODY SCAN

ANXIETY

Why Mindfulness is so Important

Mindfulness legitimately holds the power to truly reshape our brains and enhance overall brain function. Regular practice has been shown to improve memory, stress response, learning, and emotional regulation. Mindfulness can also reduce activity in the amygdala, the part of the brain responsible for processing fear, leading to a decrease in anxiety. Essentially, mindfulness builds a more balanced and resilient brain.

Meditation, a key tool in mindfulness, is particularly effective in calming the mind and body. When we're stuck in survival mode, often trapped in fight, flight, freeze, or fawn responses, meditation provides a way to bring us back to a state of calm. Our sympathetic nervous system is often overactive due to stress, and meditation helps activate the parasympathetic nervous system, inducing a restful state.

In today's society, with an overwhelming focus on constant work and productivity, many people find themselves stuck in survival mode. For generations, particularly Baby Boomers and beyond, burnout has become a widespread issue, as the constant drive for success often leaves mental well-being behind. Mindfulness and meditation offer a much-needed way to break free from this cycle and restore balance to our lives.

Perhaps one of the only positives of social media is that it's allowed a lot of people to connect and see that others are seeing these patterns and trends and that others are thinking like this too. Social media allows people to express themselves more, even about their spirituality and allows people to connect.

Reflecting on my spiritual journey, I noticed that the quarantine during the COVID-19 pandemic forced many of us to look inward. With the world slowing down, people began to examine their lives more closely, questioning who they were and what truly mattered. This time of reflection allowed and motivated many people to reconnect with themselves in ways they hadn't before.

For me, mindfulness has been important to my personal and professional growth. It's made me a better person and a more empathetic therapist. I recall a particularly tragic experience with one of my clients, a 55-year-old woman who lost her 28-year-old daughter earlier this year. I had worked with her daughter, too, and in her memory, I got a tattoo to honor her life. I still see her mother as a client, and through this experience, I've seen how grief can profoundly challenge spirituality. Yet, it is often in these moments of loss that our spiritual beliefs and practices become our strongest source of comfort. Mindfulness and spirituality, in these times, can serve as a lifeline, helping us get through the darkest moments of our lives. Earlier in my career, I would have judged myself for how I cried with my client at times during sessions. But now I feel I can stay present and not judge myself for how I may be in that moment.

Anyone can choose the path of mindfulness at any point in their life, and my in-laws are a great example of this. Raised in the Catholic Church, they no longer attend services, but they've embraced meditation after my encouragement. It's been incredible to witness their journey toward mindfulness and how it has become a meaningful part of their lives. I believe this is a trend we will continue to see more of as people search for ways to connect with their higher power in a more personal, intentional manner.

Our brain operates at different levels of activity, and meditation is one of the best ways to reach a state of calm. When we are calm, our brain is operating at a balanced frequency.

The main brainwave states are beta, alpha, theta, and delta. These develop as we age, with alpha being the state we experience during sleep. Meditation helps us reach a state between alpha and beta, where we're awake yet deeply relaxed. In this state, we are calm enough for healing to take place while being able to avoid falling asleep. When we enter these brainwave levels, our bodies and cells can regenerate, resulting in healing and restoration.

During meditation, various parts of the brain work together to process thoughts and emotions, facilitating neuroplasticity, the brain's ability to change and adapt. As you practice, your ability to focus, regulate emotions, and make decisions is strengthened. The prefrontal cortex, responsible for logic and rational thinking, plays a key role in this process, helping you respond to challenges with greater emotional control.

The medial prefrontal cortex is the part of the brain responsible for empathy; it helps us relate current experiences to those from our past. This area of the brain also distinguishes between people we are connected to and those we are not. Our brains naturally shift between focused concentration and moments of distraction. Through meditation, we can rewire the way the brain operates and enhance the connections between its various regions. As we practice mindfulness, recognizing and addressing harmful thoughts becomes easier, allowing us to reshape our thinking patterns.

Mindfulness is a protective barrier against emotional stress in relational conflicts and can help you feel more confident in expressing yourself. One of the four pillars of Dialectical Behavior Therapy (DBT) is interpersonal effectiveness, which focuses on providing tools to strengthen relationships, make new friends, and maintain healthy social connections.

For example, I love my friend Phil, who tends to interrupt others, which can sometimes turn people off. I explained how mindfulness can help him become more patient and improve his listening skills. This has had a positive impact on his communication, especially at work. Mindfulness isn't just a personal practice; it has clear social advantages as well!

Take time to pause for yourself as well. Stepping back, even briefly, can be a beneficial way to reset. I use this practice regularly, and the beauty of it is that you can do it anywhere, even if just for a few minutes. You don't need a large time commitment to breathe deeply and tune into whatever aspect of mindfulness resonates with you.

For me, these pauses have been essential to navigating everything I've experienced. Without taking these moments throughout the day, my balance gets thrown off, and I can quickly become overwhelmed or irritable. It's incredible how these little moments add up and have a significant impact on overall well-being.

The more in tune you become with what's happening inside of you, the better you can get at pausing at the right moment and giving yourself space to prevent an emotional outburst, whether at yourself or someone else. This pause period is what is called a *window of tolerance*. Something pushing you beyond this window can trigger a fight-or-flight response. The more you practice mindfulness, the wider your window of tolerance becomes. Over time, you'll be able to tolerate more without being easily triggered. As a result, the little things that once set you off will no longer have the same impact, making life feel more pleasant and manageable.

Mindfulness is a great tool for stress relief. Distress tolerance, another key pillar of DBT, is equally important. In a society that often feels stuck in survival mode, many of us are burnt out and struggle with tolerating stress. Many of us are aware of the mental and physical toll that chronic stress can take on our bodies, and having mindfulness tools to manage it can significantly improve our overall mental health.

History of Mindfulness and Meditation

The history of mindfulness and meditation stretches back centuries with roots in ancient concepts. Meditation, mindfulness, and yoga all have deep historical foundations. The concepts we associate with mindfulness today were explored by early Greek philosophers such as Aristotle, Thales of Miletus, and Epictetus. Epictetus, for example, famously wrote, "What concerns me is not the way things are, but rather the way people think things are" (Pursuit of Happiness, 2023).

In ancient China, Confucius also presented a mindful approach to life. He created eight steps for learning and self-cultivation, which have since become interconnected with Chinese culture (Confucius, 2016).

These eight steps include the following:

- *Investigation of Things*
- *Extension of Knowledge*
- *Sincerity of Thought*
- *Rectification of the Heart*
- *Cultivation of the Person*
- *Regulation of the Family*
- *Order in the State*
- *Peace throughout the Land*

The ability to change one's condition or situation through altering thoughts and attitudes is a concept deeply rooted in Buddhism. In Eastern traditions, meditation and mindfulness are often the primary forms of spiritual practice, as even the Buddha himself meditated. Buddhism and its teachings have also been practiced for centuries.

Mindfulness *can* be a spiritual practice, but this is entirely up to your discretion. Many people use mindfulness alongside prayer and meditation to seek enlightenment or connect with God or a higher power. However, mindfulness is versatile and can be adapted to meet individual needs. There are no strict rules or judgments. Whatever works best for you is perfect!

Mindfulness and meditation have recently found a place in Western culture. In the 1980s and 1990s, Jon Kabat-Zinn played a big role in bringing these practices to Western psychology. I first encountered his work through Marsha Linehan, the founder of DBT (Linehan, 2014). A full-circle moment occurred when I got to watch a virtual training by Jon Kabat-Zinn at a conference just a few weeks before this book was published (Zinn, 1994). It was in his training that he pointed out the very simple overlap of the root word "medi" being in both "medicine" and "meditation". *insert mind blown emoji*.

My Mindfulness Experience

I will describe to you what led up to what I consider my most serious anxiety/panic attack. In July of 2018, I was living in my current townhouse, my daughter was about three and a half years old. During this time, I started to confront the reality of my upbringing, which hadn't been ideal. Earlier that year, my sister and I attempted to hold a serious intervention with our dad to get him to stop drinking, but it didn't go as we had hoped. Six months later, things took a turn for the worse, and my dad was arrested for assaulting his wife while he was blacked out drunk.

When I found out, I received a call from my stepmom informing me that my dad had been arrested and was being released from jail that day. I didn't know how to handle it, but instead of processing my emotions, I went into autopilot mode. I went to my stepmom's house to collect his belongings, then tried to go to the jail to pick him up. He wasn't ready for release yet, so I ended up going to my mom's house instead. There, I broke down. I couldn't hold it in anymore, and I started crying and reflecting on everything about my father. Cue the panic and anxiety attack.

It felt like everything in my life was starting to make sense in the worst way. The weight of it all hit me all at once. I knew I needed to seek formal therapy to process the trauma because I felt like I had reached my lowest point. I didn't end up seeing my dad. Thankfully, my husband and uncle took his things to him, so I didn't have to. I spoke to him a couple of times on the phone, but all I could manage to say was that what he had done was crazy. My mind was overwhelmed with dark thoughts, including suicidal ideation.

When I had my child, I promised myself I would be completely different from my parents. I decided I would not repeat history, despite history having that natural desire to do so. But when those darker thoughts surfaced, I realized something needed to change, and I couldn't do it on my own. Whether through therapy, medication, or both, I knew I had to do something to shift my mindset. The lowest point of mental health is when you don't want to be here anymore, and it's crucial to pull yourself out of that line of thinking before it drags you even further down.

At first, I think my ego didn't want to admit that my mind needed help. The negative self-talk and judgment I carried from my upbringing had built up over time, and eventually, it got to a point where I felt like I was broken. I was scared, so it felt discouraging and frustrating as I searched for help.

I was stood up by several therapists from different practices before finally receiving a direct referral from my neighbor. In January 2019, I met Sharon, my first therapist, who led me through my very first guided meditation. At that point, I had been estranged from my dad for six months. I walked into that session and immediately started sobbing as I shared my story. At the end of our conversation, Sharon suggested we do a five-minute guided meditation together. It was incredible. In just those few minutes, I was instantly pulled out of fight-or-flight mode.

After that session, I finally understood what people had been talking about when they spoke so highly of meditation. Experiencing the power of it firsthand was a true "aha" moment for me. I had meditated on my own in the past, but never in a serious, committed way. No one had ever guided me through a meditation, and having someone do that for me when I was so emotionally flooded and overwhelmed was incredibly helpful. It was a unique experience I hadn't had before. Afterward, Sharon mentioned apps like Insight Timer, and the possibility of having guided meditations available to me at any time intrigued me.

I started using the app for guided meditations in between therapy sessions, and it was exactly what I needed. Even now, I still use it from time to time. While I often choose to listen to music to relieve stress, if I take the time to sit down formally, I turn to the app for support.

I started going to therapy weekly, and soon after, I did some genetic testing where they swabbed my cheek to test for medications and ensure that any treatment wouldn't interact with my DNA. This helped guide me in choosing the right medications for my extreme anxiety and PTSD reactions. I needed something to help manage the overwhelming anxiety and grief I was carrying. I committed fully to the process, and within just three months, I began to feel like I was finding clarity amidst my PTSD symptoms and trauma.

Mindfulness played a huge role in my newfound clarity. The word "clarity" really resonated with me, which is why I decided to integrate it into the name of my practice. Now, when people think of me, they think of clarity, and I find that so rewarding and fun. It's amazing to know that there are people who follow my social media and have sought therapy for the first time or tried mindfulness and meditation based on my posts. That means everything to me. Social media has the power to encourage people to try different techniques and normalize the process of healing.

Sharon and I only worked together for six months before she left to start her own practice. I continued therapy at the same practice and eventually met my next therapist, Jolyce. What was especially helpful at the time was that Jolyce was also a parent, unlike Sharon. Jolyce's daughter was just a year younger than mine, and she brought a real understanding of the challenges of motherhood. She was able to offer different perspectives on things like mom guilt and other tough issues I was facing that I needed to work through.

In the summer of 2023, Jolyce started using a new technique with me called EMDR—eye movement desensitization reprocessing—more on that in a later chapter. It was still a relatively new technique for her, so I kind of became her guinea pig during her training, but it worked. She's good at what she does. EMDR helped me immensely in processing my childhood emotional neglect and the struggles I had with feeling responsible for others' emotions.

I'm about to begin focusing more on the grief aspect of my trauma in EMDR, but in the meantime, Jolyce has already started helping me grieve the end of my relationship with my dad. She's been guiding me through the realization that my father wasn't emotionally present in the ways he could and should have been. Unfortunately, in the summer of 2023, my father was arrested again for the same exact thing as before. He's allegedly been sober since then, but his history has repeated itself, and I've known for several years now that I want no part of it.

I share all of this to encourage you not to abandon your practice, even if you stumble. If you fall off track, that's okay. I encourage you to get back to it. Return to your mindfulness practices and techniques, whatever they may be. When something triggers you or trips you up, remember, those tools are still available. It's easier said than done, but once you've learned how to use them, it becomes easier to return to a place of clarity and peace.

Mindfulness has taught me to let go of control, and that being mindful gets easier over time. Take a pause and remind yourself of the things you can still control. Don't be hard on yourself if you don't get it perfect; that's not helpful, and the goal is non-judgment. Once you've practiced for a while, getting back into it isn't as hard. It's all about taking that first step and starting again.

SOLAR PLEXUS CHAKRA POSE

Solar Plexus - Triangle Pose with left hand up

The solar plexus chakra is located in the upper abdomen, and is associated with power, self-esteem, and personal will. As someone who has suffered from low self-esteem for most of my life, this is an important pose that I utilize often.

How to Apply Mindfulness to Your Past

We often hear phrases that push us to leave the past behind. "Let bygones be bygones," they say. Or a similar Spanish variation, "Pasado, pisado, y superado."

But why do we keep trying to shove our past out of our lives? Almost as if we were hiding it. Does it shame us, scare us, challenge us, all of the above, or none of the above? Whatever the reason is, we often look to remove ourselves from our past when our past plays a significant role in our present.

What you go through, whether it's good or bad, makes you, *you*. It's your story and journey; as the protagonist and storyteller, you choose how to share it. Some may take things to heart and narrate a story of peace and balance. Others could try to remove themselves from it and allow a story of shame, guilt, and instability. Without being mindful, the story you tell yourself—about yourself—can have a serious negative impact on your life.

In many cases, I see the deterioration of individuals' quality of life as a direct result of how they tell their stories and define themselves. At the end of the day, this is how you see the world. It's your perspective. The energy you put into the universe is what the universe will give you in return!

It's an endless cycle, and if you define your story as one of regret, shame, or any other negative feelings you're trying to push away, you'll get the same. Taking a negative stance on your story can lead to diseases, disorders, sickness, and a steep decline in self-esteem, which is why I believe it is so important to cultivate a more positive outlook.

We're all going through it. We all have baggage, we all have traumas, and we all live in our past. Here, you have two choices: confront the issue or try to escape it by shoveling the past behind you and keep going with your life like nothing happened.

Spoiler alert: the only way out is through. But you knew that, didn't you? The real question is *how? How* do you go *through* it? Well, I'm glad you asked…

I am convinced that changing the lens through which you see life doesn't require a heavy toolbox but one single tool: *mindfulness.* Applying mindfulness to your past will help you think and go about it differently, preventing the festering and growth of negative feelings and providing you a chance to heal. Despite everyone having individual trauma, everyone's pain is different in size, shape, and form. Your healing needs to be tailored to *you.* So be gentle. Acknowledge differences between you and others, and acknowledge your feelings, needs, and wants. Acknowledge yourself as you are, and when you do, be kind. You've been through it! You deserve to cut yourself some slack because you've been trying your best. Is that "best" still not what you want? That is okay. There's no rush.

Mindfulness takes time and practice, but it will help you reshape your story and guide you toward your goals. Once you start practicing mindfulness in your day-to-day, you begin retelling your story in a non-judgmental way. This is because you are aware of the past, and you use it as a resource to help you understand your present and, later on, your future.

When applying mindfulness, you ask yourself the five Ws—what, when, where, who, why—and, finally, ask, how? Pay close attention to your "whys" and your "hows," which are the things that will show you the behavioral and cognitive processes that lead to your decision-making, feelings, and ideas. And I know, I know. You may have asked yourself those questions once or twice before, but you didn't get clear answers. Give it more tries! Some eggs are harder than others to crack. Talk it out with yourself, with loved ones, or with a professional. With whomever you speak, speak with honesty and heart about what you know and don't know, about what made you feel great and what made you feel like a bum. Talk with honesty about every aspect of yourself, not mean, just honest. Don't attack yourself. Help yourself.

I know that for some people, being kind to themselves is difficult and might feel alien or impossible. I know it because I've been through it too. Believe me when I say that developing kindness toward yourself is hard! And because I know it's hard, I decided to write this book to give you the resources you need to succeed!

Meditation is an oldie and a goodie. Practicing loving-kindness meditation (guided options for this in Chapter 3) toward your self-esteem and to others can help you feel better and be able to move past the trauma.

I think I've suffered from very low self-esteem for the majority of my life, and if your past story is extremely negative and has shaped your self-esteem, it's difficult to see clearly. Our vision becomes dark and full of negative emotions that, when unacknowledged, prevent us from healing our past wounds. Using mindfulness and tailored meditations like loving-kindness can help you build up your self-esteem and heal from past wounds. Once they start to heal, you'll start to feel lighter and better about yourself, your past, your present, and your future. Then, you'll become your mindful self.

Avoiding confrontation with your past to prevent the pain of healing limits us to one single position, one role—the role of the victim. Through this mentality, we get stuck in the past and the trauma around it, blocking us from seeing anything beyond the lenses of *that* negative experience. This way, the trauma covers us completely and stays within us, affecting our present the same way that it did our past.

In moments of absolute obscurity and overwhelm, we must remain mindful and remind ourselves of the things that ground us. We are always safe in the present moment. Thinking back on what we're grateful for, the little things that bring us joy, and the love and kindness surrounding us can shed light on our dark times. In the light, you'll find new ways and healthy paths to overcome lingering trauma.

When trauma has us stuck in a position of pain and unbalance, mindfulness helps us escape from trauma's thick and small walls. I believe mindfulness to be a powerful tool to help us break free from the feeling of being trapped by trauma. Our bodies can feel this tension as if we were in physical distress. Our bodies and minds are so connected that they leave clues for each other's feelings. Pay attention to what your body tells you, and draw connections to your feelings in those moments.

Between all of those physical sensations, there could also be stress, anxiety, and intrusive thoughts telling you there's no hope and you

are forever doomed by those past experiences that traumatized you. If you are wondering, "Am I ever *not* going to feel this way?"

I am here to tell you YES! Yes, you can feel more than just the pain of the wound. Yes, there is light at the end of the tunnel. You don't have to feel this way forever, but you do need to explore your past mindfully and reshape your perception of the past to improve your present.

Eastern Influence of DBT and Other Therapy Practices

To learn how to apply mindfulness to your past, you can do three exercises: observing, describing, and participating.

In moments of cloudiness or when overwhelmed, observing and identifying things around you can quickly ground you and calm your nervousness. Observing events, emotions, responses, and what's happening in your body in a non-judgmental way is what the *Clarity Wellness Six Core Principles* prescribe.

Describing what you see, how you feel, or the situation itself can be helpful to ground you. However, sometimes, identifying how you're feeling can be paralyzing, or you might not even have the words for the emotion.

Here, we can use another oldie but goodie: the emotion wheel, first proposed in 1980 by Robert Plutchik, is a visual wheel-like diagram of basic emotions, followed by more defined complex emotions. Utilizing this tool when unable to express how you feel may free you through rhetoric. It will give you the language to express your feelings. Later, it can also help when retelling or processing your traumatic experiences.

WHEEL OF EMOTIONS

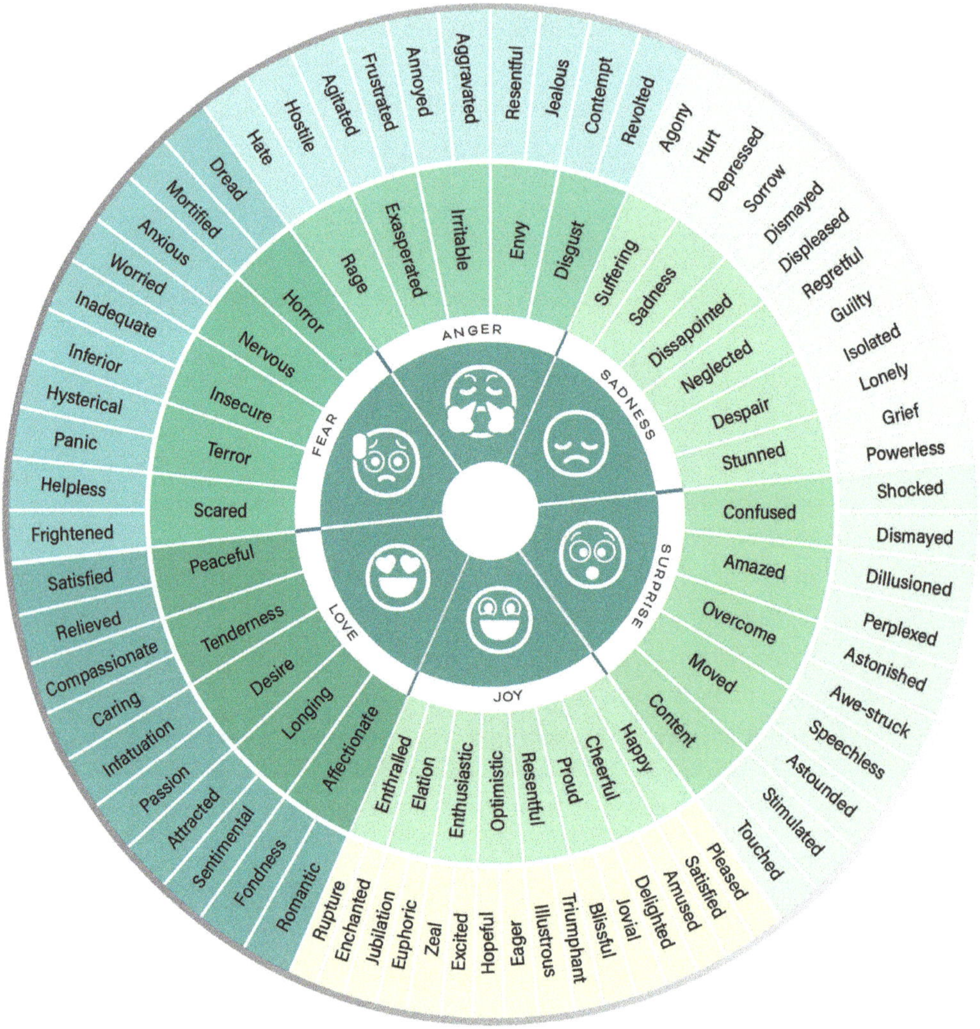

the Wheel of Emotions

The ability to apply verbal labels to behavioral and environmental events is essential for both communication and self-control. That's why I think utilizing the emotion wheel will help describe what's around you more accurately and objectively. In it, you see basic emotions at the center of the wheel, and as it expands, the feelings become more defined and detailed. So, if your basic emotion is sadness, it could be possible that your more detailed emotion could be grief, boredom, loneliness, bashfulness, apathy, etc. Using the emotion wheel will give you the language you need to retell your story and reprocess your traumas!

Participating is also a great way to stay mindful, present, and grounded. However, you must remember that said participation can not be overshadowed by self-consciousness. While participating, it is of utmost importance that you fully immerse yourself in the activity or event in a non-judgmental way, which also means pushing yourself to do it even if you don't feel like it!

Watch out for self-consciousness, the self-critic, and the overthinker. They have teamed up with your ego to prevent you from changing, evolving, and self-improving. So, regardless of the reasons these little voices in your head tell you, you have to push yourself forward, and that won't always feel comfortable. Our comfort zone is there to support and protect us, but it is not a space that allows us to grow or develop new skills.

You will have to get comfortable with being uncomfortable. And as crazy as it may sound, it's liberating! Letting go of control and embracing the change—*the new*—will send you flying like a bird, free of the pain of past traumas.

How to Apply Mindfulness to Your Past

Clarity Wellness' Six Core Principles

Now that you know *what* mindfulness techniques to apply, let me show you *how* to use them in your life. Remember, acknowledging that something exists is just the beginning of the healing journey. Some of the techniques may be more difficult than others to master. That's just a part of the process.

For now, let's unpack Clarity Wellness' six core principles on applying mindfulness to your past.

1. *Non-judgment and Openness*

For you to not be judgmental, you first need to acknowledge that the judgment exists and that you have the power to choose to buy into the judgment or not. Our brains naturally develop parameters we want to attain based on our childhood, education, experiences, things we see, and even things we assume, and then we use the parameters as a means to compare ourselves to peers. If you are unsure when you're being self-judgmental, pay attention to your language. How many times do you say, "At this point, I should have X," or "I should do X," or "I should be X?" Be careful with "should" statements, as we commonly use them to discredit our present experiences, compare ourselves to others, and judge ourselves.

With judgmental statements and vocabulary, we create a false image of ourselves based on the negative feelings the comparison leaves us with. But why do we put ourselves in that position in the first place? One in which we will be hurt. For this, we need to consider whether our parents are reinforcing this negative idea or expectation of us, our

support system, or someone else close to us. This influence cements the negative ideas into our self-consciousness.

Sometimes, the impact is overt—after your report card comes in, your upset parent says, "Susie's son got an A, and you got a B. What happened?!" This creates an expectation in your self-consciousness. It unlocks a new parameter by which you can judge yourself, and whether you realize it or not, it sticks around with you—unless you apply mindfulness to detect, dissect, and eliminate it.

Other times, the impact is more subtle—you are on the school's soccer team but don't love it. Your parent is hyper-competitive, pushing you to do more even when you don't want to and judging you if you don't. Though your trauma and negative expectations are not attached to one particular experience, they build up from several instances in which you felt belittled. Here, the judgment forges you over time and sometimes becomes difficult to identify.

If you are in a situation similar to this, take a moment to pause and observe the situation you are in without labeling it. During this step, you're not rating the situation as good or bad; you'll just state it as a fact. One of my favorite DBT principles is "sticking to the facts" of what is being observed and accepting them.

Separating our judgments from our observations is a practice meant to be repetitive. We must rewire our brains to think differently, but they often resist the change. Practice leads to success!

2. Lean In, Don't Avoid

Eastern philosophy and DBT have an interesting overlap on this principle. Both aim to highlight the truth because "the only way out is through." Whether you believe in a higher power or not, mindfulness directly related to spirituality has been shown to be a practical approach to mastering leaning in rather than avoiding.

Mindfulness doesn't necessarily have to be spiritual, but mindfulness does come from spirituality, especially Eastern spirituality. However, DBT was designed to be secular and intentionally non-denominational to increase inclusivity for non-spiritual individuals. Mindfulness itself is a spiritual practice, but the DBT skills are heavily based on these Eastern principles. Anyone can practice it.

When I first started going to therapy, I realized I had been avoiding processing my childhood experience, and then everything hit all at once. My dad got arrested when my child was just a toddler, and during that time, things became a little too much to handle. My glass was full and spilling over! So I had a breakdown that hit me in the face with enlightenment—I understood. Of course, it's spilling! I have been avoiding closing the water tabs and paying the utility bills. I have been avoiding confronting my traumas and healing from them. I have been avoiding going through the pain.

But pain is painful. We must create a process of retelling our own story so it's not *so* painful to deal with. We become so attached to negative beliefs about ourselves based on the trauma we suffer that we start to lose sight of who we are. Then, we believe our trauma's coping mechanisms to be a part of our personality when, in reality, it's just a defense mechanism. Defensiveness leads us into a hole of self-pity, guilt, anger, and victimization; none of these feelings opens space for us to grow. Instead, they cage us in our insecurities using our judgmental parameters as the law.

Whether it's through EMDR or talk therapy, retelling and reframing the story of your trauma—*your story* will help you process your experience more healthily. This will empower you and give you the means to regain control over that situation and your present. Reintegrating the trauma back into our lives requires us to clear out some of the junk that has been stored in our bodies—shame, guilt, and judgment—and the best way to let it all out is through language. Verbal or non-verbal, your voice—your language—has power, and with that power, you'll find the resilience you need to overcome your trauma. Remind yourself that you are safe in the present, pause and reflect, and choose to expand your resilience against pain.

3. Non-attachment to the Present While Staying in the Present

Revisiting our past can be triggering and make us feel like we are experiencing our trauma all over again. Think of our brains as wired computers that create responses based on previous experiences, similar to how artificial intelligence engines learn from each input received. Here, our brains' perception can be unreliable, so we need to rewire the cables with mindfulness to lead our perception into reality rather than what we're feeling in the moment.

When you release your attachment to the present moment, you release the traumas that hold close to your body, mind, and spirit. This helps you recognize that you're safe to continue your healing process and assures you the trauma isn't happening in the present. It happened in the past, but that does not mean it has to define you. *That* experience that we so dread to look back on didn't change who we are for the worse, but maybe it did for the better. You make that choice, and in those decision-making moments, while reprocessing, you'll find much personal empowerment and gain back ownership of your experience so it doesn't affect your present. This is where our third principle comes into play: to separate us from the feeling of reliving a traumatic experience.

Re-evaluating every so often allows room for change and improvement. Do not resist the change. Embrace it! As you do, you'll find other aspects of yourself that may require healing or adjacent traumas that influence your healing, and I want you to know that that's okay. We, as emotionally complex beings, are not linear, and our progress will be recursive. We will need to revisit previous life lessons, experiences, and traumas to process new ones. We are everything, everywhere, all at once—just like the movie! Having access to previous experiences as a reference, the new one can feel smaller because, through mindfulness, you have built resilience and strength to overcome traumas.

Go slow, define your own pace, and take each moment at a time— just one trauma, one day, one thing at a time, or, as the kids say, "not doing too much."

"One day at a time" may be such a popular group program slogan that it's practically a cliche, but it's true! We live in a dynamic and fast-paced society that encourages hustle culture more than it does mental health, and it can certainly be overwhelming. That's why I recommend slowing down, sticking to a simple routine, avoiding planning too far in the future, re-evaluating, and readjusting every so often to allow flexibility and room for change. This way, you will apply our fifth core principle "effectively."

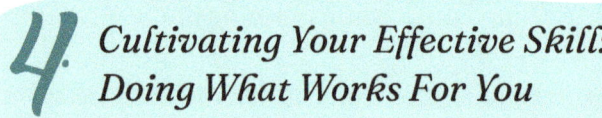

4. Cultivating Your Effective Skill: Doing What Works For You

Coined by Marsha M. Linehan but heavily employed at Clarity Wellness Solutions, "cultivating your effective skill" means doing what works for you without judging whether it's right or wrong. Instead, this skill will help you align your body-mind-spirit and support you through your personal growth journey (Linehan, 2014).

We often confuse having control of a lot of things with being proactive. But that's not quite it. Needing to control most, if not all, aspects of your life is characterized by anxious reactions, while being proactive propels you to go with the flow and stay mindful of the present moment. While being proactive, you are letting life unfold exactly as it's supposed to. For those who believe in a higher power,

letting things unfold as they are supposed to means trusting your higher power has your back and the path opening in front of you.

Even if you don't rely on a higher power, there's one within you guiding you—your gut. So trust it! If you're feeling anxious about a particular situation, it's because you probably feel out of control. Give in and let control go. Your goal now is to have a peaceful path, one full of balance and healing, so let the tensions go and join the flow.

This might be easier said than done, but take your time to find what truly resonates and works for you. You need to be open to adjustment and comfortable with change, because change never ends. A technique or skill you discover now to help you slow down might become obsolete after some time, so re-evaluating what works for you consistently is of great importance.

As we change and grow as humans, our interests change; likes and dislikes, beliefs, mottos, and the tools we use to heal change as well. So keep up with your body-mind-spirit operating system updates; they will help you navigate your past, present, and future.

This and all adaptation, relearning, and reevaluating processes have no room for shame in them. As long as a tool is working for *you* and it's effective for *you*, no one can judge your journey; only *you* can. We are creatures meant to evolve, regardless of what our lizard brains tell us. Change is good. Change is positive. We don't have to avoid it completely.

If you feel like you need help, ask yourself: What's effective? What works for me? In the end, that's all that matters. You can do this on your own, on your own time, but if you want help, therapy is here to help you figure out and identify your most effective tools.

There's no rush or deadline for when you need to get better; you choose the pace. Ideally, you would want to take it slow. There's certainly not a magical cure to healing, nor is there a concrete answer to how long your healing process is going to take. Nobody knows or can predict a healing process time frame; that's just how it is. It just takes time, and we must be ready to invest time in self-improvement.

So, take your time! Don't be afraid of slowing down; your goals won't go anywhere. One way to slow down right now? Take a moment to listen to or read the lyrics of Billy Joel's song, "Vienna." The arts always find ways to show us exactly what we're feeling and make us feel heard. Ironically, Billy Joel is one of my dad's favorite artists. Reflecting on an actual positive memory highlights the duality of man, and also why I like DBT so much. Dialectical literally means acting through opposing forces. Many emotions exist at the same time, and this is an example of such a complex idea. So here you go, Dad, this is for you, if you end up reading this. In his song, he sings:

> *Slow down, you're doin' fine.*
> *You can't be everything you wanna be before your time.*
> *Although it's so romantic on the borderline tonight, tonight.*
> *Too bad, but it's the life you lead.*
> *You're so ahead of yourself that you forgot what you need.*
> *Though you can see when you're wrong.*
> *You know you can't always see when you're right (Joel, 1977).*

So don't be afraid! Don't be afraid to lean in, change, lose control, re-evaluate, or readjust. Life will do its thing.

If there's one thing you can trust, life, the world, and the universe will do their thing. They aren't conspiring against us. They're just existing and creating life. We, as humans, get to experience their majesty by

adjusting and readjusting—learning and relearning. Even now, in my late 30s, I've had to do a lot of readjustments from methods and practices that worked for me in my early 30s. What worked for me then doesn't necessarily work for me now. I'm going through different experiences, and I have learned about myself through applying mindfulness to my past. By now, my old techniques are obsolete, so either I tune in and adjust them to my present experience or discover a new technique more suited to my present self.

Let go of the fears that prevent you from pivoting into a new direction or re-evaluating your structure. They no longer serve you. But I'm with you, it's hard. Letting go of fears, implanted in the first place to protect us, can be challenging, especially when you don't know where to look or how to analyze the information you find. That's what therapy did for me. It helped me recognize when a past method doesn't work for me anymore and when I needed to implement shifts, and it can do the same for you.

5. Get Back to the Basics

Let's define the basics, shall we? According to Maslow's Hierarchy of Needs, our most fundamental needs are eating, sleeping, and movement (McLeod, 2025). Before we dive into the specifics of our basic needs, I want you to do a self-scan and ask yourself, "Am I getting enough sleep?" or "Am I eating balanced meals?" Mindfulness starts here with acceptance of the truth. You don't have to subscribe to diet culture or be a fitness guru. It's just about being mindful and finding balance and moderation. Now, let's break them down and incorporate some self-reflective questions:

Eating

Remember our mindful exercises? This is where we can start applying them. Start by observing your current habits: Are you eating in

moderation? Overeating or undereating? Do you have an irregular eating pattern? Are there external factors influencing your eating habits? Are there internal factors, perhaps? Ask yourself as many questions as you need. Some of the most important questions to answer are not listed above. Think and reflect objectively—remember to be kind to yourself in this process.

Then, move on to describing. While eating, take a moment to appreciate your food, to enjoy it. Smell the aroma and identify flavors, pay attention to the colors and appearance of your food, and taste it. Have your meal in a quiet place where you can sit down and focus on your meal. Slowly take your first bite and notice the thoughts that come to mind. Pay attention to the memories and emotions that arise and separate them from what you are doing. Build a relationship with food that's loving and accepting of your boundaries. Enjoy your meal. This has been particularly helpful for me since I have Crohn's disease. I have to be mindful of what I eat in general, but slowing down has helped me appreciate what I *can* eat.

Mindfully participate in your eating. One of the biggest parts of applying mindfulness to eating comes a long time before we even sit down to eat the meal. It goes back to when we were grocery shopping. Food doesn't just calm down the hungry hormone. It affects our whole body, including our minds and spirits. Our nutrition can affect even our moods! That is because 90% of our serotonin is stored in our gut, meaning our gut health can either positively or negatively impact our mood. Avoiding inflammatory foods has recently been found to help with depression, along with avoiding unnatural sugars and highly processed foods. Next time at the grocery store, choose whole foods, fresh fruits, and veggies. Some foods proven to have the same nutrients as some anti-depressants include salmon, strawberries, oysters, Romaine lettuce, mussels, watercress, and cauliflower.

Similarly, some foods produce anxiety, and others help prevent it. Caffeine, processed and added sugars, alcohol, and refined carbs—

such as pasta, white rice, and pastries—are some foods and drinks you should avoid while mindful shopping. Instead, you can try chamomile, green tea, turmeric, dark chocolate, or yogurt.

Sleeping

Now, let's observe your sleeping habits. Maybe you would want to start with basic questions like, How many hours of sleep are you getting at night? Is that number in the healthy range according to your age? Are you taking naps? Are you oversleeping? How do you feel after you wake up? How do you feel when it's bedtime? Then, let your mind think freely about your sleep, try to find patterns, and pay attention to your emotions. Let the questions run, and learn more about yourself.

The connection between sleep and health is real. That is because how we sleep at night directly affects how we feel and perform each day. Sleep is as natural as blinking your eyes, but it should not be taken for granted. If you're not getting enough sleep, it could negatively affect your mental and physical health. Sleep deprivation leads to mood shifts, irritability, concentration and attention problems, failures in judgment and executive decisions, impairments in brain function and hormone production, elevated anxiety, depression, weight gain, dementia, and OCD.

So, make sleep a priority in your life. Build a sleeping routine that works for you and gets you enough hours of sleep. Try to stay on schedule, go to bed at the same time each night, and wake up at the same time each day. This may take a bit of practice to nail down, but if you're having issues falling asleep, you can try a few things.

Breathing techniques are another oldie but goodie I love to recommend. The *4-7-8 breathing* can help you relax and sleep faster. For this technique, you will breathe in for 4…hold for 7…

exhale for 8. Breathing can also be combined with bodily movements to increase your sleep ease. Yoga is one of the tools proven to help destress and sleep better throughout the night. Yoga encourages the practice of breathing patterns and body movements that release the tension built up in your body.

Other tools that improve your sleeping hygiene include meditation and mindfulness. While meditation enhances melatonin levels and assists the brain in achieving a state of relaxation, mindfulness may help you maintain focus on the present moment and prevent preoccupation feelings before falling asleep.

If you struggle to wake up, let natural light in! There's no better way to start the day than with a ray of sunshine full of vitamins. Feeling and seeing sunlight first thing in the morning has been proven very beneficial for your circadian rhythm. So don't sacrifice your sleep, even when life gets busy. Try not to skip the important hours of rest. Your future self will thank you.

My favorite tip? Make your bedroom comfortable! Make your bedroom your sanctuary. A place that resembles your goals and yourself. Bring in soft blankets, perfect temperatures to ensure a calming atmosphere, and pleasant candles or essential oils. Aromatherapy is another tool to improve your sleep health. It utilizes essential oils to trigger the senses and help you ease your mind. Some relaxing scents that encourage sleep are lavender and jasmine. Pick the one you like the most! There are many different ways to harness the effects of aromatherapy, such as misting them onto your pillow, dabbing them onto your wrists, or adding them to a diffuser.

Relax. Utilize imagery to visualize a place that makes you feel happy and calm. Think about all the specific details—construct your world. What's the weather like? What are you wearing? Who is with you? Picturing a place that helps you feel relaxed can keep intrusive thoughts away. When we are tired and restless, we are more prone to get burned out, irritable, and even depressed.

Restorative sleep is vital for your health. After a good night's sleep, you're more alert, able to think clearly, and have better control of your emotions. However, when sleep is disrupted or inadequate, it can lead to increased tension and irritability. Not getting enough sleep can also impair your mind, moods, and memory by building up metabolic waste in the brain.

Disruptions of your REM sleep cycle are both a cause and an effect of depression. If you wake up in the middle of the night multiple times a week, the restorative session your brain goes through is disrupted. It is important that, besides sticking to a regular sleep schedule and improving your sleep space, you also prevent the consumption of alcohol and caffeine several hours before your bedtime.

If nightmares keep you from sleeping or wake you up at night, practice relaxation techniques and coping skills. Progressive relaxation consists of tensing a group of muscles as you breathe in and then relaxing them as you breathe out. Practice deep breathing exercises. Take a deep breath in through your nose and breathe out through your mouth. Take advantage of guided meditation. This will keep you focused on the present moment. Putting on relaxing music and soothing sounds can release the tension and help you fall asleep more easily.

On your time awake, work on changing the narrative. The nightmare doesn't have to follow you beyond your dreams into your reality. Whenever you have a nightmare, or if you get recurrent ones, you can work to actively change the way you perceive them. Write down in detail all the events that transpired in the nightmare, but when you get to the end, write a different ending. Write an outcome that will give you a sense of peace and resolution. Then, throughout the day, continue to rehearse and relax using the techniques given as often as possible. At night, visualize the entire dream with a new outcome before falling asleep.

Dreams, I feel, can be very spiritual, especially when our loved ones who have died come to visit us in them. My grandfather, before he passed away, said he wanted to have a conversation about dreams with me, and sadly, we never got to have that conversation. He has only come to me in dreams a few times over the years since he has passed, but when he does, I feel such a sense of comfort. Perhaps another reason why I'm so big on sleep is that I feel that everyone should have a chance to see their loved ones, which can't be achieved in dreams unless you get a good night's sleep.

Movement

I'm sure you know what's next: your self-reflective questions. The most important thing to ask yourself is, are you moving? Are you applying movement to your day-to-day life? More than just walking to the kitchen, the bathroom, or the office next door? This is probably the hardest first step. Choosing to start exercising is something most of us struggle with, and even worse, trying to maintain it. However, exercise is effective in treating current symptoms of mental illnesses, such as depression, anxiety, substance abuse, eating disorders, sleep difficulties, and stress. Plus, it's free.

To incorporate movement into your routine, start by opening a 30-minute window every day for exercising in which you know you will be consistently available. I know you would love to say that you forgot, but I won't let you, and you shouldn't either! Set alarms and hold yourself accountable. Thirty minutes ain't that long anyway. You can do it.

You could invite a friend to the gym, go for a run, or exercise outdoors; having a training buddy helps with accountability. From there, build up a routine that works for you. It can start with something small, like planning to go for a walk around the corner after dinner. It will help you digest your food and make you feel refreshed.

76

We also need to change the way we view exercise. For movement to help us with our mental health, we must turn physical activity into a mindful experience. Find what you like! I found that I really enjoy rowing, and now I look forward to my time on my row machine.

Look Up and Listen. Instead of staring at your feet as you walk or exercise, look up at everything around you. If you're in a gym, look at the machinery; people are all working toward the same goal—self-improvement. If you're outside, pay attention to the landscape, greenery, and sky surrounding you, especially in a city area. Listen to the sounds of nature and humanity, and take in your environment audiovisually, like you're in a movie. Allowing ourselves to be present to sounds can change our perspective of the world and our realities.

Use a Mantra. If you find your mind wandering, bring it back to the present with mantras such as "I am at peace, I am calm," "What I'm feeling is just a feeling," and "All is well in my world." Find a mantra that speaks to and serves *you* and your purpose. Use vocabulary that's inclusive for you and represents you.

Breathe. Again? Yes, again. Always practice and stay mindful of your breathing; it is the easiest, most reliable tool, as we can use it in almost any situation—maybe avoiding underwater affairs. While practicing movement, connect your breathing to the pace of your feet. Walk slower than your "normal" stride and notice the tiny details that can be missed when in a hurry. How your feet feel as you move up a step, how the wind blows against your skin, and all the scents you feel. Mapping out your route ahead of time can ease the pace. That way, you won't have to worry about building a path; you'll just walk it.

Walk Tall. Good posture can help with your breathwork by opening your chest and stretching the muscles. So reach your head up to the sun like a flower and walk with confidence in who you are.

Leave the Phone at Home. I know this one might be difficult, especially for safety reasons, but if you are going on a walk around your neighborhood or any other space where you feel safe, try leaving your phone at home, in the car, or turn it off and put it on your bag. Disconnect from technology during your mindful walks, and remain present in your activity. Take this time for yourself.

Movement fosters and promotes a sense of accomplishment and the ability to complete tasks because it stimulates the nerve growth factor release, giving new connections in the brain through new brain cell growth. In the same way, exercise releases endorphins, a mood-boosting neurochemical in the brain, that has been proven to lessen the symptoms of depression. The most significant effects of exercise are increased self-esteem, better life satisfaction, and decreased negative thoughts.

You can practice movement in many different ways; however, studies show aerobic exercises, in particular, are as beneficial as standard antidepressants (BMC Psychiatry, 2024). Moderate-intensity aerobic exercises such as walking for 20-40 minutes three times a week can significantly alleviate many symptoms of depression, including a decrease in sleep disturbances and improvement of the general mood.

Physical activity raises core body temperatures, creating a feeling of relaxation and relief. Consequently, it gives its practitioner a sense of self-efficacy while stimulating the release of nerve growth factors in the brain. Yet, if you want to take it even further, consider practicing movement outside. Moving your body anywhere will be beneficial, but getting some sunlight is an added bonus. Sunshine promotes healthy blood flow in the brain and triggers the production of vitamin D, which plays an important role in maintaining brain health. Vitamin D stimulates the growth of nerve cells to preserve memory and executive function and sustains mood. But remember

GETTING BACK TO THE
BASICS CHECKLIST

to keep your skin healthy against UV light. Use your SPF and be mindful of your time in the sunlight. Some individuals may be less resistant to the sun's rays than others. Please do not be like my friend's father, who passed from melanoma because he disrespected sunscreen.

If you're still wondering why you should apply these mindful techniques, it's because I believe you deserve to feel your best. There is hope, even when your brain tells you there isn't. Nevertheless, I don't recommend diving into your trauma re-evaluation until you are at least at a medium level of mastering your basics. This is where everything begins. So, let's make sure you're settled and comfortably healthy with your eating, sleeping, and movement routines.

6. *Try Different Techniques*

Navigating your healing journey alone can be difficult, especially without the knowledge and expertise a professional would have. Sometimes, having that other person to help guide you can help you feel safe again. Re-evaluating and readjusting to retell your past story can be difficult and downright terrifying when processing trauma. That's why I am so adamant that having someone walking the road along with you can be so encouraging.

It can be tough to go back and relive trauma to process it. It is not an easy feat. That's why having a trained professional guiding you through your journey is so much easier. A therapist also helps you to acknowledge your avoidant tactics. They help us see those little things that are oblivious to us or we can't pinpoint—they help us name those tactics and keep us accountable. At least my therapist does that for me, and I do the same in my practice.

It's okay to ask for help, and it can be to our benefit. That's what therapists are here for. Because I err and my therapist keeps me accountable, I am such a proponent of accepting the help and going to therapy. At the end of the day, we're just human beings. Even as a therapist, it is difficult for me to recognize all my avoidant tactics. An outside, experienced perspective is always helpful in showing the full picture. Just like a training buddy for exercising, a therapist is our mindfulness buddy. We all have our own trauma set and biases. Even therapists benefit from therapy, and I don't think there's anything wrong with that. Rather, it shows our recursive nature.

Seeing a therapist a couple of times a month can help you stay on your routine. At least, it has been effective for me because through my healing process, I discovered therapy works for me, and even now, I still attend personal therapy sessions a couple of times a month. Through these recurrent meetings, it is always easier to re-evaluate what works for me and what changes to my routine could benefit from. This cognitive process is simplified when the person you are talking to has been with you through it. They'll have an outside perspective on how said routine suits you and be able to provide objective feedback.

I don't think I would have made as much progress in my journey of healing and self-discovery without my therapist. She has been the one to call out when previous techniques become obsolete and provided me with new ones I never thought of using before, because my biases would prevent me from thinking outside of the box.

From self-reflection, academia, and guided conversations in therapy sessions, I have found that there are a variety of modalities for applying mindfulness to your past.

Some of them include:

Somatic Healing Methods

These provide a holistic approach to focus on the mind-body-spirit connection. These methods address your traumatic experiences' symptoms and push you to embark on a transformative journey toward recovery, resilience, and greater balance. Applying somatic healing methods will allow the access and release of emotion and tension stored in our bodies.

Through awareness of bodily sensations, somatic healing is a hands-on, physical approach that goes after the root causes of physical and emotional issues, granting us the chance to release our trauma and stress. Some of the most popular methods of somatic healing include yoga and meditation, massage therapy, breathwork, dance and movement therapy, acupuncture, craniosacral therapy, and somatic experiencing—an approach developed in the 1970s by Peter Levine that looks to learn from internal physical experiences.

Eye Movement Desensitization and Reprocessing (EMDR)

EMDR is a type of psychotherapy that helps process and heal from traumatic memories. This practice encourages the patient to focus on trauma memory while experiencing bilateral stimulation, normally rapid eye movements. Through these movements, we can rewire the brain's negative connections with traumatic events.

EMDR relies on the model of Adaptive Information Processing (AIP) since it describes how the brain stores information and memories. Developed by Francine Shapiro, PhD, this practice recognized that the brain stores normal and traumatic memories differently, furthering our understanding of how to heal from trauma.

This practice has been proven to be beneficial for individuals who struggle with mental health. That is because EMDR helps reduce distress, intense emotional negativity linked to trauma, and symptoms of PTSD like nightmares, flashbacks, and hypervigilance. Similarly, it improves self-esteem, as well as overall health and well-being. EMDR helps you process and integrate traumatic memories back into your life in a healthy way. For this, ideal candidates for

EMDR include victims of physical or sexual assault, neglect or abandonment, war, natural disasters, or those who have suddenly lost a loved one.

When I first started my healing journey, I realized that I felt responsible for my parents' emotions, as well as my siblings and other relationships. I felt responsible for everyone's emotions. That was because growing up, my dad was kind of using me as his therapist, right when he and my mom were getting divorced. He would call me, a few martinis deep, and just weep, wanting me to console and counsel him. All of this while I was around 24 years old and was dealing with my feelings as a result of their separation. I was vulnerable, and his expectations didn't help my case. It made me feel almost as if I didn't do a "good job" at making him feel better, then it would be my fault he was feeling that way.

Knowing that feeling was likely linked to past experiences, I tried EMDR to tackle the traumas related to my feelings. I tried it, and it was tremendously effective. Through my sessions, I was able to reprocess those memories and solidify the idea that you are not responsible for other people's emotions. This method built a strength within me that empowered me to accept my values and roles. I am not a weak person, and I can retell this story more positively.

Practicing EMDR permitted me to talk to my past self and explore boundaries. It's okay to say no. It's okay to have your limits. It's okay to have boundaries. There were many times when I felt like I wasn't holding boundaries enough, and talking to myself and a professional deeply helped me reprocess.

So, from now on, talk to yourself. Talk to your younger self with your current perspective. Help your past self navigate through that stressful situation with the knowledge you have now. It's kind of like being your own parent, work, or counselor guide; those moments, talking to your past self, are raw and real. Keep it real to yourself!

Internal Family Systems (IFS)

IFS is an individual or group therapy practice that is designed to help adults who display a wide range of secondary clinical effects from trauma, such as dissociation, somatization, and affect dysregulation. The practice sees the human brain as composed of various "parts," and theorizes that said parts are representative of memories, emotions, thoughts, behaviors, and even those representations of early childhood trauma. It recognizes and addresses individuals as a combination of subpersonalities or families within each person's mental health.

IFS looks at our different perspectives, interests, memories, and viewpoints and draws upon mindfulness, self-compassion, self-acceptance, system theories, multiplicity of the mind, and trauma theories. At its core assumptions, IFS holds each practitioner as inherently capable of healing while acting as our intuitive, emotional, and intellectual center. This model revealed many benefits for its practitioners, such as understanding and managing emotions effectively, healing from past trauma and negative experiences, improving their interpersonal relationships, increasing self-awareness and self-compassion, as well as developing a greater sense of peace and overall well-being.

In IFS, there are what are called the 8 C's and 5 P's of self. I did not know that Clarity was one of the 8 C's of self, according to IFS, before I named my practice. But now that I know this, I want to try IFS both as a client and as a therapist. (Add it to my list of goals for my future self.)

Some exercises you can practice along with IFS include:

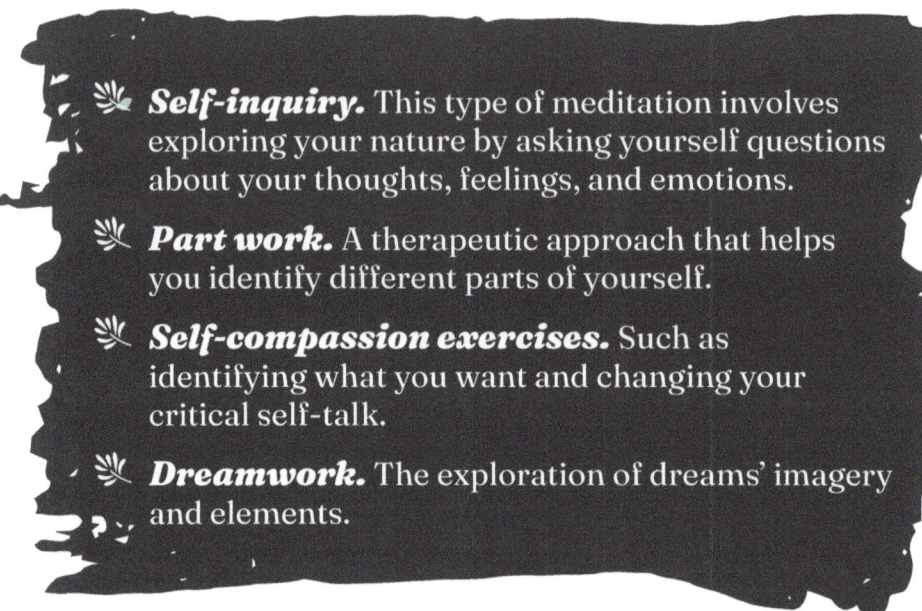

- **Self-inquiry.** This type of meditation involves exploring your nature by asking yourself questions about your thoughts, feelings, and emotions.

- **Part work.** A therapeutic approach that helps you identify different parts of yourself.

- **Self-compassion exercises.** Such as identifying what you want and changing your critical self-talk.

- **Dreamwork.** The exploration of dreams' imagery and elements.

Emotion Freedom Technique (EFT), Tapping, Psychological Acupressure

EFT is an alternative treatment for physical pain and emotional distress that, by tapping the body, can create a balance in our body's energy system and treat the pain. EFT developer Gary Craig believes that disruptions in your energy flow cause negative emotions, past traumas, and pain. So, similarly to acupuncture, EFT focuses on meridian points to restore the body's energy balance, alleviating symptoms that negative experiences or emotional trauma may have caused.

While acupuncture uses needles to apply pressure to the meridian points, if you are afraid of needles, you don't have to worry! EFT uses fingertip tapping, and you can repeat the tapping as many times as you need until you feel a significant reduction in the issue's intensity.

Though there are 12 meridian points on both sides of the body that connect with internal organs, EFT only focuses on nine points: the pinkie side of the hands, connected to the small intestine; the top of the head, connected to blood vessels; eyebrow, to the bladder; side of eyes, to the gallbladder; under the eyes, to the stomach; under the nose, to blood vessels; chin, to the central vessel; the collarbone, to the kidneys; and under the arm, to the spleen.

Think those are your only options? Think again. Other exercises that can strengthen the mind-body-spirit triune connection include, but are far from limited to, yoga, meditation, Tai Chi, QiGong, dance, nature walks, journaling, and art therapy.

Types of trauma therapy we practice at Clarity Wellness Solutions

At Clarity Wellness Solutions, we offer a variety of therapy practices that better accommodate your needs. Our therapy approaches include mindfulness-based therapy, cognitive behavior therapy (CBT), dialectical behavior therapy (DBT), and interpersonal therapy.

Cognitive Behavior Therapy (CBT)

This style of therapy includes exploring both your past and present with a particular goal in mind. It focuses on changing negative thought patterns and behaviors. CBT has demonstrated its effectiveness for a range of problems, including depression, anxiety disorders, alcohol and drug use problems, marital problems, eating disorders, and severe mental illness.

Our approach includes making sure we take the time to fully understand you, your past, and your present moment. While practicing CBT, the therapist and client build a strong relationship that allows a clear understanding of the client's story and historical background. Simultaneously, the therapist can initiate conversations with the client to discuss the present moment—Where are they now? What kind of issues are they running into at present? As therapists, we constantly look to find patterns in the present because more likely than not, they are rooted in the past.

In sessions, we balance the present and past levels in our conversations. CBT doesn't look to carve out the past but to identify the interrupters in our lives and explore where we think they stem from. Through these conversations, we will reframe those experiences from a non-judgmental standpoint—it won't always be positive, but it can be more often than not.

To get a positive reframe, we first have to let go of our negative biases. This will take time, so instead of trying to turn the negative into a positive, we begin by meeting in the middle.

Getting to a more neutral place first will ease your progress toward a positive one. Each client has their situation they are dealing with, but if you're struggling to change particularities, try focusing on getting a neutral stance.

Reframing is just like changing—scary. But if you're feeling stuck or paralyzed before the change, remember how much that past experience is affecting you and how much you deserve to feel better. In moments like these, neutral statements come in very handy because then the change is *less of a change*—it isn't as abrasive, as harsh. Instead of doing jumps that are way too big, we'll take smaller steps so the jump feels more attainable and less daunting.

If this is something that you can relate to, or you have been stuck in a negative thought loop, and want to try out neutral statements on your own time. Check out some of these neutral statement exercises:

Neutral Statements: On the Way to Positive Affirmations and Self-Love

(Could be applied to past, present, or future)

I have what I need to heal within me.
I have the power to change my world and the world around me.
I believe in myself and my ability to learn and grow.
I am doing my best to take care of my body physically.
I am worthy of celebrating because I am a good person.
My life has an abundance of love and happiness.
I let go of negative beliefs and negative self-talk.
I say no when I need to.
I am working on setting healthy boundaries.
I embrace all my fears and use them as ways to improve.
What I give to the world is what the world gives to me.
I am working on self-love every day.
I accept my imperfections.

Once you've tried them out in the wild, and if you'd like to discuss the results of your neutral statements, please call or scan the QR code below to talk to me or one of our Clarity Wellness Solutions professionals.

Dialectical Behavior Therapy (DBT)

This is a style of CBT that teaches people how to be mindful, develop healthy ways to cope with stress, regulate emotions, and improve relationships with others. DBT is a practice for people who experience emotions very intensely, for it is common among individuals with borderline personality disorder (BPD), but is effective with a variety of mental illnesses. This modality emphasizes the importance of non-judgment, openness, and understanding. Therapists apply the four pillars of DBT: mindfulness, distress tolerance, emotional regulation, and interpersonal effectiveness.

I believe that just having somebody else outside of my mind and brain, saying, "Hey, why don't you look at it this way?" makes the change so much easier. Personally, having a therapist helped me learn how to view my past, not let it impact my present, and return hope for my future. So here, I'd like to open a space to shout out to my therapists and all therapists out there for helping me accomplish this level of balance and for doing what you do. They are the reason why I do what I do. I want to be that person for others because I think I need it so much; I don't think I'll ever stop needing it, but that's okay. As we change, your session frequency also changes, and can always be adjusted to your current needs.

Above all, always remember to be kind to yourself! I say it all the time to my clients, I've said it before, and I'll say it again.

Be kind to yourself.

That is the most important thing to keep in mind when you're exploring your traumas and looking for healing. You can trust yourself, you can trust CBT, you can trust DBT. Therapy has made me realize that we have everything within us to heal. It's just a matter of clearing away all the crap that comes from trauma. You can have a clearer present—more of a present in the *present* if you're willing to do the work to heal from the past. Then, you'll find CLARITY.

What part of your teen years would you change?

....

....

....

....

....

....

....

....

....

....

....

....

....

....

....

....

....

....

....

....

....

....

Letters to Yourself

There's nothing like writing longhand to work through certain concepts and ideas. If you've ever written a letter to yourself, then you're familiar with the concept. It can be encouraging to have words on hand, from yourself, to encourage you when times get tough. You know yourself best, so there's no one better to ask for advice! Below, I'll share a letter to my past self, then encourage you to do the same in your journal. It's just for you, no one else.

Letter to Past Meg

My dear,

It truly gets better. I'm here to spoil things in the best way, to give you the hope and strength to carry on when you feel like giving up. The unknown does not have to be paralyzing. I know you wish you were psychic, so that you could determine that it will all work out. I'm here to tell you just that.

You end up facing your extreme fear of childbirth, and it goes really well! And you only have to do it once because you and your husband realize you can only handle one child, and that's okay! You're on the same page about it. And you do get married kind of young at 24, but thankfully, you picked the right one, and he is your absolute rock through all of the ups and downs that dealing with your family brings.

It's a pretty bumpy ride at times, but you do heal. You find the best therapist thanks to your neighbor/BFF. You're introduced to mindfulness and meditation, and it changes your life for the better. You really do achieve the goal you have had since high school, and that is starting your own therapy practice. It doesn't go as you would think, so just be open to anything and everything.

Owning your business is hard work but it is worth it. So yeah, spoiler alert, it does all work out. You recently discovered that your grandma is actually your step grandma and I know you have so many questions. It will be many many years before you get these answers, but you will get them.

Please keep on keeping on, lean on your friends, Allison, Dakota, Hannah, and especially David. They will all be there in your darkest hour. I love you.

Love,

Future Meg

Write your own letter to yourself.

....
....
....
....
....
....
....
....
....
....
....
....
....
....
....
....
....
....
....

HEART CHAKRA POSE

Heart - Dancers pose

The heart chakra is located in the center of the chest, near the heart of course. This chakra is associated with love, compassion, and emotional openness. A personal struggle for myself has been that emotional openness. I feel like I can learn to love myself in this pose.

Chapter 5

How to Apply Mindfulness to Your Present

There is work to be done to heal the past and promote a mindful future. A future that is more aware and peaceful—less judgmental. A future that leads to a more fulfilling life. It's about being mindful of your present moments. Being more aware of what you are doing in the present.

There's no finish line for this. There is no set goal. It's not about, "If I can be this much more mindful, I'll be good." Mindfulness in the present is an ever-repeating process. It's constant work. Forever remembering. Does it feel like you are forever worrying about the future? Or are you stuck dwelling in the past? What about the present? Practicing mindfulness doesn't do this. In fact, it helps steer your mind away from these thoughts. It gently brings your mind back to the present.

One of the reasons why our minds will wander into the past or future is because that is where the ego is built. We all have an ego. It's just part of being human. We are constantly pulled into the past or

future. It is a persevering practice to bring the mind away from it and not be controlled by the ego.

When the ego gets triggered, it might react with anger or fight-or-flight. That is when we become emotionally dysregulated. The ego is what makes the judgment when you get upset or angry. Your reactions begin with the ego and its interpretations of what is happening in the present moment. It's about whether or not your pain body is being activated and to what degree.

The past comes up when we have traumatic situations we haven't tackled. Sometimes, we think we might have it dealt with, but we are just numbing it. There's a good chance that the things you are doing might not be so healthy. They might be pulling you back to the past. Those poor coping skills can make us more anxious.

Don't forget about the five Ws and your how. Pay close attention to your "whys" and your "hows." These will show us our behavioral and cognitive processes that lead to decision-making, feelings, and ideas. These skills help us focus on the present moment and let go of our attachment.

What is so good about staying in the present moment? Well, for starters, if you are anxious about the future, staying in the present moment can feel good. It helps get us back in touch with our purpose. Getting back in touch with that purpose helps us to feel safe in the present. "I am right here, right now." Staying present in the moment allows us to be a human BEING, not a human DOING or someone continually ruminating on the past or future.

My default, before therapy and mindfulness, was fear and anxiety. I was just worrying, worrying, worrying. I thought that was normal. I felt I had to worry about something if I didn't want it to come true. When I started practicing mindfulness, I felt content. I'm not worrying about anything. I'm just here. Now.

I didn't feel peace like that for a long time. When I found it, it was like, "Oh wow!" It's an amazing feeling to embrace. I would describe it as feeling normal or being human. It removes my worries and my fear. There's just peace.

It does take an adjustment period. "Oh, this is what I'm supposed to feel like to be alive?" It's worth the affirmation that you are where you want to be. You are where you should be. It's worth the effort to get back to the present moment. Your mind might think, "This is different; I don't know what this is. Don't do it anymore." As long as you are mindful of returning to that, it is so worth it.

The more we can be in the present moment, the more we can be in control of the ego. We don't want the ego to control our lives, actions, or inner spirit. We want to be in control of the ego.

A lot of my clients struggle with time scarcity. They get stuck in a loop of "There's just not enough time." They might fight for perfection because they are scared there won't be enough time to fix anything that goes wrong. Everything must be perfect in the moment. That is the ego talking.

If we can identify that, we won't face that time scarcity anymore. It is the ego that thinks I don't have enough time. But I can stay present and remember: I have all the time in the world to achieve what I want to achieve. The ego is trying to gain control and prevent us from staying present.

If the ego can control you, then the ego is going to feed off the energy of your past traumas and the worry about the future. The stronger those emotions are, the stronger the ego is, the more it can control us. Ultimately, the mind, body, and spirit are out of balance.

Everyday Mindfulness Techniques

Mindfulness can be incorporated into just about every aspect of the daily routine. I'm personally very big on routines. They are so important. This is where I recommend gradually adding mindfulness—in the every day.

Do you have a good sleeping routine? What is your morning wake-up routine? How do you start your day? How you start your day is important. It bleeds into the rest of your day, painting it with the same brush. What is your work schedule like? Do you have an after-work or evening routine? This is where I need to look. Where can I incorporate mindfulness in any parts of those daily routines? Additionally, how does your weekend routine differ from your weekday routine? How can you incorporate mindfulness there? Are you still moving, eating, and sleeping enough? Is there a good balance overall?

Remember the basics from Chapter 4: eating, sleeping, and moving. Maslow's Hierarchy of Needs says our most fundamental needs are eating, sleeping, and movement (Maslow, 2019). How are you incorporating these into your life? Being intentional with these things is another way to practice mindfulness.

Do you have limits on your screen time? Many people use phones as their alarm clock, which can be a tough start to the day. We get up and look at our phones first thing. We screw ourselves up from the get-go by using our phone as an alarm clock. Limiting screen time in the morning is much easier said than done. But the more you restrict it, the better. Could you try journaling instead of being on your phone?

Is your breakfast balanced? Are you eating the meals you need? Everybody's needs are different when it comes to nutrition, but are you getting what you need? What do you need for your schedule? How can you apply mindfulness to eating? Can you slow down and take your time? Pay attention to how you pour your coffee, butter your toast, and cook your eggs. Be aware of what you are doing. Be mindful of all your senses.

When I am working with my clients, after I get all their background information and trauma history, then I try to get into what their daily routine is like. Then, we can figure out how to incorporate mindfulness into it. Can we reduce screen time? Can we go for a walk? It is one thing at a time. Something as simple as enjoying every bite is a way to stay present. It's not meditating, but being mindful of how we are doing things.

Even when you are doing things you do every day, you can still be mindful while doing them. As long as you are doing things one at a time and paying attention to your senses, you are being mindful. Take your morning routine, for example. Do you wash your face? Take the time to be present in that practice. Focus on your sensations rather than your thoughts about the past or future. Make sure you aren't going on autopilot.

What about your work routine? Do you have a commute? What does that commute look like? How are you spending that time? What are you listening to or thinking about? For many of my clients, their commute is their only time to decompress. If that is the same for you, use this time to get into a good mindset.

Pay attention to what you are listening to. What are the podcasts or the music telling you? If you turn all that off and it's just silent, pay attention to that. What comes to mind? Are you okay with the silence, or are you afraid of what thoughts might arise? That's a part of mindfulness, too. Just be mindful of your thoughts and what you are listening to.

Your evening routine is the same way. See how you can incorporate mindfulness into your evening routine. Do you cook dinner? Take the time to focus on the aromas of the foods and how they taste. And your movement routine is again the same.

When working with clients at Clarity Wellness Solutions, we regularly dive into routines like this as a part of mindfulness practice. And beyond just daily routines. Your weekend routine, too. Do you meal plan? Meal planning on the weekends is helpful so that there isn't as much planning throughout the week. Meal prepping is excellent, too, because there is no reason to have to cook throughout the week. If you are busy, busy, busy, it's a simple grab-and-go. Some of my clients could benefit from this, so they aren't neglecting their health.

What are other ways we can apply mindfulness every day in our lives?

Mindful eating is one way. Find a quiet place to sit down and focus on your meal. Take your time eating and notice as much as you can about the experience. Look at the color of the food. Smell the aroma. Feel the texture. Take your bites slowly. Notice the things that come to mind while you are eating. Pay attention to the memories and emotions that arise. Separate them from what you're actually doing.

Mindful dating is another way. This is one that a lot of people think is wild, but it's true. This is a no-judgment zone. I have a client who would be an expert on mindful dating. He keeps a journal to keep track of all his dates. Who it was and where they went. I support this so much. He keeps track of what went well on the date and what didn't go well. I think this allows you not to string someone along. It also allows you to understand and communicate what you need in a relationship when dating and meeting new people. The more mindful you are, the better you can communicate. I think keeping a journal like that is a way to be intentional about what you are looking for and need. You can sit there and break it down. To me, it's the most respectful way to go about dating.

There is even a way to be mindful while gaming. This is something I came up with because my husband is a gamer. He plays an Xbox. He's been a gamer as long as I've been with him, and the first couple of years of our relationship were out of control. He was not mindfully gaming. It impacted our relationship a lot.

I've never judged him for playing games themselves. It was when it started to impact our lives that it was too much. It's not good if the time that you're spending gaming is bleeding into other parts of your life. I've had to work with him on being more mindful about the time that is spent gaming. We don't want it to start affecting our eating, sleeping, movement, or relationships. If it's impacting your ability to get back to basics or your basic functions, that's the problem.

Gaming can be something people use to disassociate. It can be addictive and make us numb to our feelings. Where in our routine are we spending time gaming? How much time are you spending doing it? It has to have a cap on it at some point. If you are willing to be mindful about where you are incorporating it into your routine. You need to have balance. You have to track the time that you spend doing this.

What about mindful working? It can be difficult when you are new to a job, or even just the working world, especially if you have people-pleasing tendencies. It's hard to find your identity in this new stage. Let's give an example. Let's say Alice is two years into her job, and she's just finished this crazy project. Her co-workers and even her higher-ups were aware she had overworked herself and acknowledged that, saying they would make sure she didn't do it again. It's not normal. I feel like when you are new, you feel like you just have to say "yes" to everything. It is not mindful to overwork yourself.

I find a lot of my clients do that. They say, "I'm finally in this job, and I have to say yes to everything and prove myself." It's part imposter syndrome, part self-esteem. A component of building yourself up.

Be kinder to yourself and don't get stuck in the rigidity of a routine, especially if you've been working hard.

Practicing mindfulness at work is also about setting boundaries. Setting work boundaries, in particular, helps us make sure we aren't burning ourselves out in the first few years of the job. Take your time. We still have a lot of time ahead.

Are you having a weekend out drinking with friends? Do you feel like you drank too much, or you are out of control? A lot of people don't recognize that they are overindulging. Let us unpack this and ask ourselves some questions nonjudgmentally.

Do you think this is a pattern? How can you prevent that from happening next time? If it was distressing to you, let's process that. Let's unpack it. Could this happen again? What caused this to happen in the first place? To apply mindfulness, just start by limiting how much you can have. Maybe one or two drinks is all you limit yourself to.

This can apply to marijuana, too. I had a client who recognized that weed was getting in the way of school. There was another client who recognized that it helps with anxiety, but too much of it prevents them from being successful in work or school. When they told me, I said, "It's amazing that you recognize that. Thank you for bringing that to me. Let's figure out how we can have more of a balance." We go back to the routine things. Where in your routine do you usually do this? Where can you limit it? Is it affecting your body, mind, or spirit?

One thing you can be assured of at Clarity Wellness Solutions is that we won't judge you for your lifestyle or using substances. As long as it's not throwing your mind-body-spirit connection off balance, the substances you use are your business. I'm going to help you be mindful about it. From a personal experience, I drank way too

much in college. I thankfully have reined it in, and I know I prefer cannabis, but I've been there. I do still drink socially, though, but I can't let myself have more than two, or I will get sick. I think it's Crohn's disease. It's just something to be mindful of.

It can be challenging to stay mindful during unexpected shifts in the daily routine. From accidents to everyday traumas, some things happen throughout the day that can cause us to panic. What if you got into a car accident a few weeks ago? How would you practice mindfulness and move past it?

I had a client who this happened to. Thankfully, she didn't have a very long commute, but she got into a major accident on the highway. From then on, she would take the back roads to avoid getting on the highway. Being able to drive on the backroads made her feel safe driving again. Something like a car accident activates the pain body. It's trauma. Every time she drove near a highway, her pain body was activated. Being able to drive short distances allowed her to feel safe.

Then, driving short distances a lot over time and then going further distances helped her become more and more comfortable and safer. It took her about a year to drive on the major highway where the accident occurred again. She even had to be a passenger first.

In therapy, this is called exposure therapy. But it is also using mindfulness. You are aware of what sensations are occurring or rising while you are exposing yourself to whatever it may be. If it's causing a lot of fear, are you telling yourself, "Hey, I'm safe. I'm in the present moment, and I'm not in the trauma where this happened."

Our minds and bodies can be thrown back into that past, so practicing mindfulness is important. For my one client, post-car accident is where it is so important to be as present as she possibly can, so she can feel safe again. Over time, that pain body will shrink, and you can go back to your everyday life.

Did you just have a breakup? The loss of a relationship is something that needs to be grieved. If I have a client tell me they are going through a breakup, I might say, "That's awful. I'm so sorry. How has that impacted your eating and sleeping? Are you still focusing on your basics? Are you taking care of yourself? Has it impacted your other relationships?" I want to help them process their feelings.

Grief is so important and unique. Everyone grieves differently. Everyone needs to figure out how they grieve. It is okay to grieve. It may feel like there is no time—here's time scarcity again—but there is. Don't think, "Oh, there's no time for me to grieve." Yes, there is.

Everyone has time to grieve. It's important to give that time to yourself, whether you want to do it on your own, just think about it, write it down, or talk through it. I think talking through it with a therapist, or even just a friend, family member, or loved one, is helpful. Just some way to get it out instead of holding it all in. Then, address whether this is affecting your eating, sleeping, and movement. Are your relationships being impacted? There is more work to grieve that loss.

One of my clients, I mentioned her previously, lost her daughter recently, and I encourage her to still do whatever she wants to do that makes her feel connected, such as talking to her every day. She goes to the cemetery every day as part of her routine. It's a way for her to mindfully grieve because she knows she is going to be able to grieve and think about her daughter as part of her day, and then she can keep going, somehow.

There are even ways to find mindfulness in your identity through the changing tides and different seasons of your life. As I keep reiterating, I've been rereading Eckhart Tolle, from *A New Earth*, and I was reminded that it's the traumas that can make us more spiritually awakened and aware. Sometimes, it is healing from a pain body experience that makes us more spiritually awake (Tolle, 2005).

I think about an experience from my own life. In 2018, I had what I consider a mental breakdown, and I went into no contact with my dad. I felt like I was more mindful after that. I was certainly processing traumas, but it made me feel more present. It was these "aha" moments, these epiphanies, which can certainly take place at any time, but they have more of a tendency to take place after major traumas.

As you heal from things, you might come up with different revelations. You might want to try new things and change old things. As a result, people might leave your life, but new people might also come in. If you ask me, as long as you are kind to yourself throughout the process and you go one day at a time, one thing at a time, one trauma at a time (mindfully), you can be successful.

I think these things also bring in the spirituality aspect. Sometimes, they can make people question their spirituality. That's why it's easiest to just numb things and not think about them. We don't want to deal with it. "Why would my higher power let this happen?" That is hard to sort through. But, to borrow Tolle's phrases, I think it's the ego talking because the ego is stuck in the past. Knowing this, how can we reflect on how it might impact our future?

There's no explanation for a lot of awful things that happen in the world, and we need to be okay with it. That's easier said than done, but through time and trying to remain present, we can learn to be okay with it. It's just a continuous practice to come back to the present. But the more you can lean on your community and just remember that you aren't alone, the easier it will get. That is what makes things less painful to go through.

Mindfulness in the present is a skill that must be learned, and it is an ongoing process. But it is so worth it. As Thich Nhat Hanh said, "The best way to take care of the future is to take care of the present moment" (Hanh, Goodreads).

THROAT CHAKRA POSE

Throat - Cat/Cow pose

The throat chakra is naturally located in the throat area, and is associated with communication, self-expression, and authenticity. I thrive on the idea that I am a solid communicator, but low self-esteem has caused me to judge myself, and stifle my own authenticity. This pose helps me break free of that self judgment so I can express my true self.

Chapter 6

How to Apply Mindfulness to Your Future

Applying Mindfulness to Your Future

It's probably clear by now that mindfulness mostly applies to the present moment, but there are a few ways it can be applied to your future as well. The choices you make in the present have a significant impact on what lies ahead.

Let's take this back to the basics: how much quality sleep are you getting each night?

The amount of sleep you get affects how you feel the next day, whether that be through drowsiness or irritability. If we look to the future, the consequences of poor sleep can be much more serious. Research shows that chronic sleep deprivation is linked to a higher risk of conditions such as dementia. While this may seem like a distant concern for many, maintaining a healthy sleep schedule today is an investment in preventing chronic diseases down the road.

These same principles of mindfulness apply to what you eat. As someone who must be conscious of my diet to avoid flare-ups, I understand personally how intention affects the body. What you put into your body and how you care for it requires you to be mindful of your physical self. Both your actions and your choices have short and long-term effects.

When we operate on autopilot, we fail to notice when we're not being mindful. Every person's body and health needs are unique, but over time, neglecting balance in these areas leads to consequences, circling back to the law of attraction—thoughts create things, and in turn, your thoughts can create your future.

Visualization isn't just for inspiration. It's an effective tool for creating your future. By picturing what you want your life to look like, you tap into a deeper energy. There is real power in your thoughts, and being mindful of them allows you to align your actions with your desired outcomes. Picturing your thoughts and habits can help you better understand yourself and intentionally shape the future to your ideals.

Boundaries

The different boundaries you choose to enforce and advocate for yourself can be considered mindfulness regarding your future. A boundary is simply knowing your limits; everyone has them, even if they are not consistently enforced. The more you understand yourself, the easier it becomes to establish and maintain boundaries across different areas of your life.

One of the most challenging yet important areas for setting boundaries is in relationships, particularly within families. For instance, many parents don't fully consider their children to be real human beings, which can lead to resentment and conflict. Whether they are rigid or loose, families, in general, need to have boundaries.

It's up to you to determine what feels right in your interactions with others. Consider how much time you want to spend with someone, the topics you're comfortable discussing, and how much of yourself you're willing to share. Boundaries help define your comfort zone and protect your well-being, ensuring that your relationships support you, rather than drain you. Everyone has different preferences when it comes to these limits, and that's perfectly okay. What's important is recognizing and respecting those healthy boundaries.

A common critique of mine on social media when I post about boundaries is that it is so shameful to go no-contact with my father because he is, after all, my *father*. People assume that since I went no-contact with my father, I'm going to encourage all of my clients to go no-contact with their parents. Well, that is what we call counter-transference, and thankfully, I am aware of those feelings and process them with my therapist before I let those feelings influence what I say to clients. I truly do my best to help my clients explore every avenue of healing and communication before going no-contact. That decision is personal and is always the client's decision exclusively.

Advocate for Your Present and Future Self

I know firsthand how difficult it can be to advocate for yourself, especially when setting boundaries. I've struggled with it greatly, and I truly empathize with how intimidating it can be. This is precisely why understanding your limits is so vital. Setting boundaries is one of the best ways you can advocate for yourself. The more mindful and aware you are of the boundaries you want, the easier it becomes to implement them.

Remember that we're not focusing solely on the future because that can make things too ego-driven, and we want to avoid that. With that being said, if you can be intentional and mindful about the boundaries you want in your life, you're setting yourself up for the future you want, keeping your mind, body, and spirit in alignment. Most importantly, it allows you to say "no" when pushed to your limits.

Those who have trouble saying "no" often have loose boundaries. Loose boundaries often include a deep fear of rejection and acceptance of abuse held by those with low self-esteem. Loose boundaries sometimes cause people to overshare, something I have unfortunately learned through my father.

While boundaries are important, they can become too strict as well. Rigid boundaries are held by people who are a little too closed off, as many tend to be overprotective of personal information and keep their contact at a distance. Rigid boundaries can prevent people from authentically interacting, and that can place a huge strain on relationships.

Knowing your limits and securing mutual respect for yourself and others is essential to working toward healthy boundaries. Establishing boundaries in the present helps shape a better future by allowing you to advocate for yourself and what you want (or don't want). We touched briefly on applying boundaries to your past in Chapter 4, but it's important to remember that boundaries also influence what lies ahead. The choices you make now set the foundation for the future you want to create.

Boundaries are something I didn't have when I was helping my dad through his divorce from my mom. His lack of boundaries after their separation left me in a position where I felt like I had to pick up every phone call, becoming his personal therapist. Over time, I realized this was a form of emotional incest, which can have effects similar to other forms of incest. Situations like this illustrate how important it is to understand your limits in every area of life. To maintain balance and protect your well-being, you must know yourself, know your limits, and be clear about where you stand with your boundaries.

If you're having trouble saying no or instating boundaries, there are three simple steps you can follow to begin with.

1

Press Pause.

Instead of immediately agreeing to whatever is being asked of you, consider the cost of that "yes." How do you wish to spend the hours of your life that are in your control?

2

Ask yourself...

- 🌿 What will I need to sacrifice to accommodate this request?

- 🌿 Why do I want to say yes? Do I genuinely want help? Or am I perhaps looking for validation?

- 🌿 Who will my "yes" serve? Am I trying to please someone specifically? Am I fearful that by saying "no," I may let someone down?

- 🌿 Is there someone else who can help with this responsibility?

- 🌿 Does saying "yes" honor my voice and internal values? Am I ultimately taking care of myself?

3

Say NO!

Even when you don't say "yes" with your mouth, you can say it with your body. Showing up for others when your mental health is low, answering every text and email right away, and tolerating disrespect from others are all ways we give in to people's demands.

Whenever you say "yes" when you do not want to, you say "no" to yourself. Be quick to identify this, and you'll soon be able to shift your actions to align with your mind.

What Do You Put in Your Body?

What you put in your body has both short and long-term effects. On autopilot, we often don't fully pay attention to what we consume. Mindfulness applies to the ways we treat our bodies, whether it's the food we eat, how much sleep we get, or how we care for ourselves in general. All of these elements have immediate effects, but with many of us rushing tirelessly through our daily routines, it's easy to fall into habits driven by convenience that distract us from being mindful.

Convenience culture encourages us to hustle and work endlessly, but this approach may not benefit us in the long run. Fast food, for example, is an easy and quick solution when we're on the go. When I was driving around to do client home visits in previous jobs, I had my fair share of fast food, and I'm sure it contributed to my eventual Crohn's diagnosis. This kind of convenience can be addictive and harmful to the body, so it's essential to be mindful of your routine and reserve convenience for those rare moments when it truly serves you. For many, this is a difficult balance to maintain, but you'll be rewarded with better health in the long term.

Pay attention to where in your routine you're reaching for shortcuts and conveniences without being mindful of their impact. Ask yourself if this part of a routine benefits you. Is it aligned with the best interests of your mind, body, and spirit? When you can pinpoint these moments without judgment, you can redirect your attention in real time, and that's what mindfulness is all about.

We face countless choices every day, and while the power of choice is freedom, it can also be a double-edged sword. We can make decisions that support our best future by pausing to reflect on our options.

If you don't rush through your decisions and take the time to reflect, it can empower you to make better decisions in the moment. Consider the impact of each choice on your trinity. By taking that moment to pause and reflect, you can ask yourself questions like, "Should I choose something a little healthier?" or "I've had time to play this game for 30 minutes, not an hour, should I take a break now?" These are small but meaningful ways you can integrate mindfulness into your routine.

Your Future Through the Law of Attraction

The Law of Attraction is the idea that you can bring whatever you desire into your life through the power of your thoughts. It's the energy behind our thoughts and the potential to manifest our desires. Some people see this as a way of communicating with a higher power through prayer (if you believe in one), but science, metascience, and mental health interpret it in various ways.

For me, the Law of Attraction is simple: you can attract what you want into your life through the energy behind your thoughts. This concept has a spiritual element, as it can serve as a direct link for communication with a higher power. Regardless of your beliefs, there's an undeniable energy in our thoughts, and that energy can bring about real changes in our lives.

I remember hearing about Mike Dooley when I was around 20 years old, and I was fascinated by how "thoughts become things." One part that stuck with me was his 21-day manifestation story. He led a visualization activity where he provided mini scripts for different aspects of life, allowing you to sit and visualize each one (Dooley et al., 2012). I loved how you could get so specific, especially since I hadn't been exposed to this idea much before.

At its core, the Law of Attraction is about being mindful, intentional, and aware of your thoughts (some might even call this prayer). The power of your thoughts and the energy behind them is very real. If you're interested in exploring this concept further, I recommend checking out the aforementioned docuseries, *The Secret* (Heriot, 2006).

Earlier, I mentioned how I manifested where I live, and it all started with intention. My husband, Bryan, and I were very visionary about what we wanted in a house. We became mindful about creating a vision board for our future home and family. I remember being young and having diverse friends, and I wanted my daughter to have that same experience, surrounded by people of different backgrounds. Despite moving to a predominantly white area, we got incredibly lucky with our block—it turned out to be very diverse. (Shout out to "Bracey Lit Drive"!)

I believe this speaks to the power of intention. I would often reflect on my own childhood experiences with friends, and the strong desire I had for my daughter to have that same diversity in her life helped me manifest it for her. Some might call this practicing mindful thinking or prayer. Prayer, particularly in Christianity, is deeply rooted in intention.

You can link the spiritual aspect of your mind-body-spirit trinity to both prayer and meditation. However, this can be tough, especially for those who struggle with mental health issues like intrusive thoughts or OCD. It's important to remember that intention doesn't mean that every single thought will manifest exactly as you envision. Similar to an example in *The Secret*, just because you think about an elephant doesn't mean one will appear in the room. If you struggle with intrusive thoughts, they can feel scary, but it's important to remind yourself that just because you think of something doesn't mean it will happen. What matters most is your intention.

When it comes to trauma and PTSD, if you're experiencing a flashback or intrusive thoughts, please don't assume that just because you thought of something, it's going to happen again. That's not manifestation or visualization; it's a symptom of PTSD. Ruminating thoughts aren't a sign that something bad is about to occur; they're your brain's way of trying to protect you.

If you've ever heard the phrase, "Don't believe everything you think," it's referring to intrusive thoughts. These are not thoughts your brain wants to have. Instead, they're protective mechanisms that, at times, can become overly active; the mind wants to shield you, even when you no longer need that level of protection.

Being intentional about your thinking helps you focus on what you want and directs your energy toward creating a positive future. When you approach this with mindfulness, you engage with your mind, body, and spirit on deeper levels. What kind of future do you want to attract in each of these areas? Let's explore a few exercises that can help you curate the future you desire.

Mindful Exercises: Training Your Brain to Craft Your Future

Creative Visualization

Visualization is the process of clearly imagining exactly what you want, often through meditation. If you're not familiar, this is about using your mind in the best way possible. Some people might call this a daydream, and it is perhaps a VERY intentional daydream, but it is specifically a dream where you are consciously creating and guiding your vision. To make it effective, getting as specific as possible about what you want is important.

While visualization is similar to daydreaming, daydreams often happen spontaneously, with thoughts just popping in. With visualization, you are actively creating and guiding your intentions, making you the conductor of your desires. Envision whatever brings you a sense of freedom, and genuinely harness that feeling.

For example, visualize yourself traveling the world, visiting the most beautiful destinations, where money is no obstacle. Mike Dooley's visualization guides include exercises like this, where he encourages you to picture yourself traveling to your dream locations (Dooley et al., 2012). Don't worry about money; focus on the experience while visualizing every detail. He suggests writing down where you want to go, who you want to meet, and what the journey looks like.

Are you staying in hotels or sleeping on trains? How are you getting there? How long will you be traveling? What's the purpose of your trip? Are you traveling for fun, adventure, or self-discovery? Are you spending a year exploring the world solo? Take time to thoroughly analyze these questions in your mind. You are essentially writing your latest memoir, and the more detailed you get, the more enjoyable and relaxing the process becomes.

Take a moment to sit down and think about what you truly want. This requires slowing down and dedicating time just for yourself. While you might feel like you're not doing anything productive, it is about setting aside the outside noise and distractions. We don't often make time for this. Giving yourself that space can be easier said than done, but persistence pays off. The more time you dedicate to it, the more likely your dreams will happen for you.

Giving yourself the time and space to slow down and do something for yourself is essential. How can you accomplish big dreams if you don't even give yourself the time to think about that future?

CREATIVE VISUALIZATION EXERCISE

Pick a goal or something that you want to attract. This can be absolutely anything in life that would benefit you and your trinity.

Focus on this goal: What does it look like? Visualize with all 5 senses.

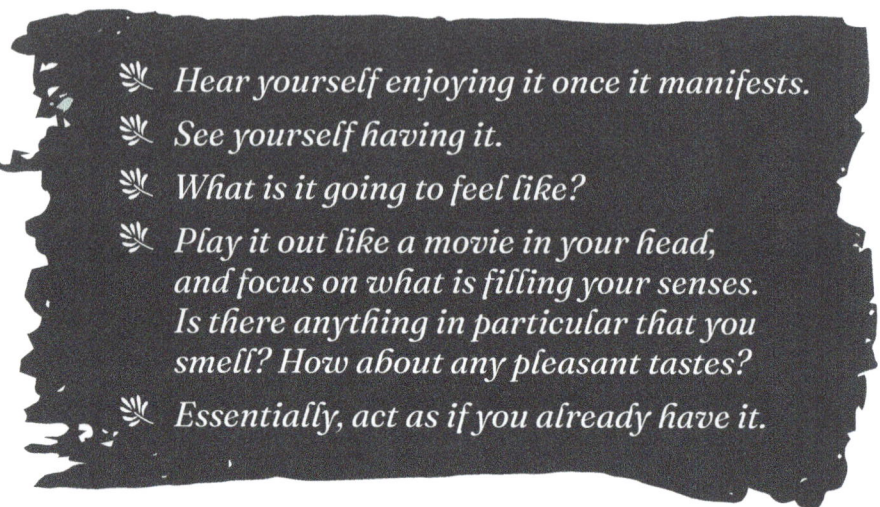

🌿 *Hear yourself enjoying it once it manifests.*

🌿 *See yourself having it.*

🌿 *What is it going to feel like?*

🌿 *Play it out like a movie in your head, and focus on what is filling your senses. Is there anything in particular that you smell? How about any pleasant tastes?*

🌿 *Essentially, act as if you already have it.*

This is an excellent opportunity to test your mindfulness. Keep coming back to visualizing this goal as often as you can. The more you return to it, the more detailed you can get with the image you create!

Your Routine

Of course, make sure the basics in your routine are covered. Are you eating enough, sleeping enough, and moving enough?

As part of your daily routine, consider adding creative visualization. Whether you're commuting to work or have a few quiet moments during your day, think about whether there are times you can use to visualize any part of your future, whether short or long-term. These small moments of focus can help bring your dreams to life, one visualization at a time.

Positive Self-Talk

Everyone has an inner voice. Think about what yours is saying to you. Is it beating you up or questioning whether you're good enough? If so, it's time to consider shifting the way you speak to yourself.

Negative self-talk can be overwhelming, especially when you're not achieving everything you want. It can have a damaging effect on your mind, body, and spirit. Reframing those thoughts takes time and effort, but it's essential to have grace with yourself along the way. How you speak to yourself is a big part of CBT and DBT. I have a client, Amy, who has very negative self-talk and inner dialogue. She has improved dramatically in the last 5 years by working with me on reframing those thoughts.

No matter what you're going through, remember that you are human and deserve to feel good and talk positively about yourself. A lot of our self-esteem depends on how we speak to and think about ourselves, and you should never beat yourself up for how it works. My neurodivergent clients are especially hard on themselves because they believe they should be doing something that a neurotypical brain would be doing. There is no "correct" way to be human. You just have to learn how your mind works and how to work with it.

POSITIVE AFFIRMATIONS FOR
ANXIOUS SITUATIONS

Visualize, Create, and Manifest

Have a little fun for yourself! Once you've carved out the time to craft your future, enjoy the process as you tap into your inner artist to manifest your dream life. Not everything has to feel heavy or serious.

Art in any form can be especially helpful for this. If you're a drawer or painter, try illustrating yourself in that future scenario you're dreaming of; this can be incredibly inspiring! You could also sing about it or express your vision in a poem or song. You can use any creative expression that resonates with you.

Circling back to visualization, picture collages are another great way to represent your future. This could be a vision board, but it doesn't have to be limited to that. You can make it as general or as specific as you want. This is your future; your mindfulness and creativity are the only limits.

Play is another fantastic way to engage with manifestation, and this is where things can get fun! Using arts, crafts, and even music is something that most of us have done as kids. This can be an easier way to do something fun for yourself because there is that familiarity factor. Lighthearted fun creates space for a more carefree spirit.

The Future is in Your Hands

The future may seem daunting, but there are many ways to take control of it. By thinking ahead and taking the time to truly understand yourself, you can make better, more intentional decisions that serve your long-term well-being.

While it's important to plan, stay grounded in the present. Don't let your ego push you to only look at what's to come; instead, focus on making decisions that create a lasting impact in the moment and beyond. Mindfulness is a personal journey, and there's no need to be perfect from the start. Have fun with yourself, honor your limits, and remember that even small actions can impact your future. Your choices today influence the life you'll lead tomorrow, and you control your path.

Letter to Your Future Self

Remember the letter-writing exercise from a few chapters back? It's time to revisit the concept. This time, looking forward. Here's my letter to you!

Dear Reader,

I'm keeping this short and simple.

It will all be worth it. All of the hard work will be worth it. Right now, as I'm writing this, I've been able to look back at how far I have come. And I still think there are more healing and joyous moments and memories to come, which is why it is worth the hard work and utilizing mindfulness to work through past traumas and regain a sense of your personal trinity. It is always okay to fall off your routine as long as you get back on at some point. But the main thing is to keep working towards your goals. The small steps lead to significant progress. And that is much more important than perfection. With continued mindfulness, you can lead a more balanced and fulfilling life. You have seen firsthand how it is possible. Now, the task is to keep it going!

Love,

Present Meg

THIRD EYE CHAKRA POSE

Third eye - Cow face pose

The third eye chakra is located in the center of the forehead, and is associated with intuition, insight and psychic abilities. I consider myself naturally insightful and intuitive, but if I'm having trouble figuring something out, I might turn to this pose. It usually encourages me to listen more.

So, Mental Health, Mindfulness... What's Next?

If you're getting started on your mental health or mindfulness journey, you should know that there is no expectation on how to get started, meaning that wherever you start—whether that's meeting with a mental health professional or implementing mindfulness on your own—it is the right way to start. There's no wrong way to begin your journey; it's about what serves you and choosing to prioritize your trinity (body-mind-spirit). So start your journey today; leave any negative judgments of the past out the door, and embrace a life of peace and balance.

Try as many different mindfulness techniques as you can! You don't have to use them all, but explore them; figure out which ones work best for you in which situations. It's up to you to figure out and decide how you want to build your trinity, and mindfulness exercises will be the necessary tools to materialize it. Use mindfulness and creativity to visualize your desired future. I don't think I could list all of the healing methods and mindfulness techniques I have tried. I was reminded of how many I have tried while writing this book. I

feel like it's the beautiful combination of everything that has led me the furthest down my healing journey.

Be Kind to Yourself

This is one of my favorite and most overused phrases. I end a lot of my social media posts with, "Stay kind to yourself!" I feel like the reminder needs to be constant for a reason. The inner critic and negative self-talk are so well programmed into us that shaking them off is tough. Your healing journey might bring up uncomfortable topics or situations. These are your most vulnerable moments. One in which your present self confronts your past self. Redirect that conversation to one far away from hate, resentment, shame, or guilt. Invite your past self in and let them explain themselves. Come to an understanding with them and accept that they are there, but only as something that *happened.* It just happened. Let your past self know not to worry; you got the wheel now, and both of you are safe. You are a different person from the past who doesn't hold grudges or regrets against yourself, and you are ready to rewrite your story.

Practice Radical Acceptance

Don't judge your story, and be willing to not be ok sometimes. It might be challenging. You might want to run the other way. You might want to avoid it. But as we established before, the only way out is through. Practice self-kindness and accept whatever comes your way. Remove any negative judgment, and I know you'll make it through. It may sound easier said than done, but with practice, it gets easier over time.

Bring Open-mindedness and Commitment

Remember that rewiring our brains takes time. Don't try to rush things. Until you've been in therapy for a solid six months, or maybe a year and a half, you won't see any progress. This journey can take months or even years. You need to be willing to do the work and commit to prioritizing your mental health.

Some people believe therapy is a waste of time—but that's the ego talking. The ego doesn't want to do the work to change or to give up control. That's why I know that if you commit this time to yourself, you will be much more successful in your mental health and mindfulness journey. It just takes a lot of time to uncover everything and work through all the past trauma and all the biases that influence your interpretation of the past.

If you are starting over in your mental health and mindfulness journey, just remember that we leave any judgment of the past or negative experiences at the door. You're a different person now, capable of forgiving your past self and letting go of judgment and resentment. Give yourself a clean start with this new knowledge, and leave behind anything detrimental to your trinity.

Get Started with Mindfulness

Remember, your healing journey starts wherever it serves you best. Explore as many mindfulness techniques as you can. Some of my favorite recommendations for mindfulness rookies include:

Visualization

It is as simple as setting a mental image. You can better connect to things you can imagine, which is especially helpful for audio sensations. Utilizing visualization as a tool throughout your mindfulness journey is vital because "[e]ven when you are not paying conscious attention to what you hear, your brain is analyzing the soundscape around you to provide clues about the nature and activity of your surroundings" (Pijanowski et al., 2011).

Journaling

The practice of putting your intentions on paper. Everyone will have a different process, but "simply writing down your thoughts and feelings [helps] to understand them more clearly" (University of Rochester Medical Center, Rochester, 2024). Journaling can manage stress, anxiety, and depression, but almost everyone can benefit from being mindful and setting their intentions toward expression.

A prompt or two to get you started:

1. What do you love the most about the current season? Include the holidays you celebrate, festive food, scents, and activities.

2. How do you feel you have grown this year? What would you like to manifest in the new year?

3. Who or what cheers you up when you're having a bad day?

4. What are some things you love about your friends?

5. Write out three things in your home that make you happy.

6. List the scents, spaces, textures, and sounds that bring you joy. How many of these can you fit into one experience?

7. What part of your teen years would you change? Were there needs that were not met? What emotions does your inner teen hold in and repress?

8. Are you proud of the person you have become so far? Do you feel like you have more room to grow? What areas do you want to grow in?

9. Write down what makes your body, mind, and spirit feel healthy. This includes relationships, habits, and ways of thinking. After creating your list, plan something every week this month that you can add to benefit your mental and physical health.

10. What is your biggest struggle with loving yourself? What is a compliment that you have trouble accepting? Reflect on the ways you show yourself love and acknowledge how healthy they are for you. How can you accept love from others more easily?

Mindful Movement

It is an interconnectedness between the mind and body. It requires "an embodied presence, anchoring our awareness to the senses of our bodies as we move through space and time" (Trepp & Sandweiss, 2023). This does not have to be a complicated process as the intention "can be as simple as standing up from the desk to stretch, taking the stairs to another floor to use the restroom, taking a moment for a snack or to share a meal, enjoying a view from a favorite window, or *going outside* and walking!" (Trepp & Sandweiss, 2023).

There are many ways in which you can try mindful movement. Some I mentioned before, like yoga and massage therapy, and others include the Chinese practice of Qigong (chi-gong) and sound immersion.

Yoga is one of the better-known practices in the US for promoting mindfulness and mental clarity. While there are varying elements among different cultures, "yoga as practiced in the United States typically emphasizes physical postures *(asanas)*, breathing techniques *(pranayama)*, and meditation *(dyana)*" (Belfer & Shurtleff, 2023).

The Chinese practice of **Qigong** (chi-gong) is a movement and breathing-based practice similar to yoga. A lot of the movements are used in yoga routines. "Qigong is both a moving and stationary meditation that opens meridians, massages internal organs, and lengthens and strengthens the musculoskeletal systems" (Mary Pinkard, 2024).

HEAL Lower Back, Shoulders, Hips | Qigong Daily Routine to BEGIN YOUR DAY (10 Min)

Massage Therapy is a practice in which the mind and body work as one, making it best for prioritizing physical well-being. Massage therapy is one tool people use to enhance wellness and physical relief, and it "involves manipulating the soft tissues of the body" (Mudd & Shurtleff, 2019).

Reiki Therapy is another healing modality to explore that works differently to reach different goals. Reiki therapy takes a lighter approach to the body while focusing more on energy healing, as it is "based on an Eastern belief that vital energy flows through your body. The idea is that a person specializing in Reiki treatment, referred to as a Reiki master, uses gentle touch – or places their hands just above your body – to help guide this energy in a way that leads to balance and healing" (Starkman & Mitchell, 2024).

Sound Immersion is a meditative practice using soothing instruments to guide body and mind into deep relaxation, relieving stress and tension, and enhancing calm. For instance, I love a great stillness sound bath—where you sit or lie down and let the sounds of gongs, chimes, and crystal bowls wash over you. Sound immersion has been found beneficial for reducing stress, improving sleep, boosting emotional well-being, improving focus and clarity, alleviating anxiety and depression, and more (L. Golsby et al., 2016). During the first sound bath I did, I was reminded that our bodies are made up of 60% water, and sound moves through water so well.

Whichever type of practice you choose to start, sound immersion is about giving ourselves a pause—this is the only way I get through the day sometimes. So take a beat and a deep breath. There's no shame in stopping occasionally, and it doesn't have to be complicated!

Start small; the simplest things can be the most important ones. Take little breaks throughout your day; don't wait until you're excessively tired or burned out to give yourself a break. Instead, add them between tasks or break them into smaller chunks if a task is too long. Process your day with awareness, and during your break, observe what's happening around you. What do you do on your break, and how do you do so? Then, come back to your routine empowered. If you need to, add your little breaks to your calendar or to-do list, but make sure you get them! I assure you it'll have a great impact on your life satisfaction.

A Beginner's Quick-Start Practical Guide to Meditation

Before we embark into meditation, keep in mind there is no ONE way to meditate—from box breathing to loving-kindness meditations, walking, or beyond. There is no particular way in which you HAVE to meditate.

But you can always start by setting the scene. It can be beneficial because you're being intentional; it's creating that intention and just really knowing what you want. So what do you want? What are you hoping to achieve in this meditation session? Once you have that nailed down, we can move along.

Here is a step-by-step getting-started guide I've shared with many clients:

 Set the scene.

You will first need to find a quiet and comfortable place to practice meditation for at least 10 minutes. Put on relaxing music, listen to a guided meditation, and add a fragrance if certain smells give you peace. Make sure the temperature in the room is to your liking.

 Breathe.

Start by taking a few deep breaths to bring you relaxation. Inhale through your nose for a count of five, hold your breath for a few moments, and then exhale for a count of five.

 Muscle Relaxation

Bring attention to your body and do a self-scan. As you go, you will bring movement and tension to each part of your body and then relax them.

- *Feet:* Curl your toes in, then relax
- *Thighs:* Flex the individual muscles or squeeze them against each other; then relax
- *Torso:* Suck in your stomach, then relax
- *Back:* Push shoulder blades together, then relax
- *Arms:* Tighten your biceps, then relax
- *Hands:* Make two fists, then relax
- *Face:* Contort your expression, then relax
- *Full Body:* Squeeze all muscles together, then relax

4. *Acknowledge Your Emotions.*

As you meditate and move your attention over different areas of your body, feelings might arise. Simply acknowledge the emotions and accept them free of judgment. Can you pinpoint why you feel this way? Let go of the need to control the emotion and continue with your breathing. Gradually bring your attention back to the room.

At this point, we have explored useful key steps to initiate your meditation practice; still, you have to keep in mind that this journey is deeply personal and unique to each one of us. These techniques, despite their simplicity and practicality, will help you build a strong foundation of mindfulness in your life. As you continue to explore and refine your meditation practice and become curious about the broader implications of mindfulness in life, remember our connection through this book. At Clarity Wellness Solutions, we're all rooting for you!

A Personal Note from Meg

As I sit here, reflecting on the healing journey that brought us together, I am overwhelmed with gratitude for your commitment to make it this far. Thank you, from the bottom of my heart, for picking up this book and investing your precious time into reading it, and for prioritizing your personal trinity.

Your recognition of the delicate balance of body, mind, and spirit aligns perfectly with the very purpose that drives me: to share mindfulness as a concept and lifestyle and show you, a clarity seeker, the benefits of this life.

By reading this book, you have allowed me to fulfill my purpose, and for that, you will forever have my gratitude. My only goal is to help you discover your true self and purpose and start your healing journey—I know I am living mine through this connection with you.

As you moved through the pages of this book, I hope you found the tools necessary to facilitate your journey initiation. It is my firm belief that bringing balance and harmony to your trinity creates a profound clarity within you that illuminates your path.

I want *you* and everyone to live their life's purpose, and I hope this book helps you achieve that. I've found that purpose comes when your inner trinity is in balance.

My sincerest wishes,

CROWN CHAKRA POSE

Crown - Tree Pose

The crown chakra is located at the top of the head, and is associated with spiritual connection, wisdom, and enlightenment. Since creating my ancestor alter, I feel more connected to my loved ones than ever before. Sometimes I will stand in the tree pose right next to that altar, and I feel like I can hear their messages.

Acknowledgements

I have to start by thanking R&R Publishing, especially Cat Lopez. Thanks to the universe and the algorithm of Instagram, Cat stumbled upon my business's page. I'm so grateful that she reached out and offered to help me write and publish my book. Once again, it is an example of not worrying about the "how" and focusing on the "what" instead. I always knew I would write a book, but I had no idea when or how. Would it be before or after I started my practice? Not until I retired? What would I write about? Obviously something mental health related, but what specifically? And where? Sometimes, I saw myself sitting in a cabin in the woods, isolated with nothing but a typewriter, and at other times, the idea of writing a book all on my own was scarier than all of my first days of school put together. I couldn't see a "how," but that didn't matter. What mattered is that I knew I would get my message out someday, somehow. Cat's process was made for someone like me, someone who has an idea but isn't sure of how they want to convey it. I'm beyond grateful to Cat and her team for making this dream of mine come true in what feels like the blink of an eye. I know this is just the beginning of a new chapter of my journey as a business owner, as a mental health clinician, and as a therapist.

Oodles of gratitude go to my husband, Bryan, and our daughter, Brynn. They are my rock and my anchor, and what keeps me going every single day. The endless amounts of laughter and love that they provide are incredibly healing. I appreciate their support in allowing me to chase my dreams of being a business owner and author. Any guilt I hold is self-induced because they are my biggest cheerleaders. I don't care if it is cliche to say, Bryan is my knight in shining armor. He has saved me from more than he knows.

Thank you to my mother and sister for attending family therapy with me in 2023, which contributed to even more healing. Thank you especially to my sister for indulging me in my search for what happened to our grandmother, Marilyn. Shout out to my first therapist, Sharon, who guided me on my first meditation, and Jolyce, who has been with me through it all but has really conducted miracles through EMDR. All of this contributed to making this book and to making me the healed person that I am today.

To my cousins Dakota and Hannah, who are more like sisters, and my uncle David, who is my true father figure, thank you for being a constant healing presence in my life. They had their own parts in getting me through my breakdown of 2018, and it is imperative that they know how grateful I am for that. My mom's side of the family is always picking up the pieces of shrapnel that my dad left behind.

To Mallory, Maria, Zoe, and the rest of my Salisbury crew, thank you for your unwavering support in this spiritual journey since college. You all made me feel like I could have fun again without judging me (too harshly..;-)) And through that, I found myself. And to Mallory's mother, Ms. Robin, thank you for introducing us to *The Secret* in 2006, which I still see the ripple effects of even today.

A special nod to all of my clients, past and present. My life has been so enriched by working with all of them. I feel incredibly blessed to have had such a diverse group of clients over the years. Each one has made me a better person and therapist. I know that so many of them are destined for great things, and I pray that they know that as much as I do.

My former colleagues, especially Luz, Maria, and Alisia. I would not have survived working in an OMHC for 10 years without them. I was privileged to share an office with Luz and consider her a mentor. Maria and Alisia started as my interns. Eventually, I brought them on to my practice for a few months before they went on to start their own practices. I'm such a proud supervisor of them both.

And to my current staff of clinicians: Malorie, Katie, Asha, Erin, Emma, and Madison. Thank you for helping me achieve my dream of "mental health support for all". We have been able to serve hundreds of clients from Maryland and Virginia. I feel like a better person and therapist getting to work with these wonderful ladies. Thank you all for everything you do!

Allen, A. P., Dinan, T. G., Clarke, G., & Cryan, J. F. (2017). A psychology of the human brain-gut–microbiome axis. *Social and Personality Psychology Compass, 11*(4). https://doi.org/10.1111/spc3.12309

American Foundation for Suicide Prevention. (2024, May 11). *Suicide Statistics*. American Foundation for Suicide Prevention. https://afsp.org/suicide-statistics/

American Society for the Positive Care of Children. (2025, January 17). *Take the ACEs Quiz*. American SPCC. https://americanspcc.org/take-the-aces-quiz/

Boston Medical Center Psychiatry. (2024, August 20). "Influence of aerobic exercise on depression in young people: a meta-analysis". BMC Psychiatry.

Brown, B. (2010). *The gifts of imperfection*. Hazelden Publishing.

Byrne, R. (2006). *The Secret*. Melbourne, Australia; Prime Time Productions.

Clarity Wellness Solutions. (2023, Apr. 14). *Body Scan Guided Meditation* [Video]. YouTube. https://www.youtube.com/watch?v=0kGJbvhbEa4

Clarity Wellness Solutions. (2023, Sept. 26). *Clear Away Fears Held in the Body - 10 Min Body Scan* [Video]. YouTube. https://www.youtube.com/watch?v=RisInecoCsY

Clarity Wellness Solutions. (2023, Sept. 20). *Connect With Your Body* [Video]. YouTube. https://www.youtube.com/watch?v=XJgMEqQUpsw

Clarity Wellness Solutions. (2023, Sept. 11). *Easing Into Mindfulness 10 min* [Video]. YouTube. https://www.youtube.com/watch?v=VMSaANtagcc_

Clarity Wellness Solutions. (2023, Mar 27). *Guided Meditation for Empathy* [Video]. YouTube. https://www.youtube.com/watch?v=KvmgwGtwGD0

Clarity Wellness Solutions. (2023, Oct. 24). *Meditation for Patience* [Video]. YouTube. https://www.youtube.com/watch?v=tllQitB-I9g

Clarity Wellness Solutions. (2022, Aug. 29). *5 Minute Guided Meditation - Accepting Failure* [Video]. YouTube. https://www.youtube.com/watch?v=bKZwd1b0lvE

Clarity Wellness Solutions. (2022, Oct. 31). *5 Minute Guided Meditation - Awaken Intuition* [Video]. YouTube. https://www.youtube.com/watch?v=NjcfPveOBxA

Clarity Wellness Solutions. (2022, Jul. 20). *5 Minute Guided Meditation - Healing* [Video]. YouTube. https://www.youtube.com/watch?v=pJs8kQDWHRU

Clarity Wellness Solutions. (2023, Nov. 16). *5 Minute Guided Meditation - Helping Others* [Video]. YouTube. https://www.youtube.com/watch?v=HhpGqERldxs

Clarity Wellness Solutions. (2023, Oct. 9). *5 Minute Guided Meditation - Mindfulness of Breath* [Video]. YouTube. https://www.youtube.com/watch?v=Ah-9GhTGF1U

Clarity Wellness Solutions. (2023, Oct. 30) *5 Minute Guided Walking Meditation* [Video]. YouTube. https://www.youtube.com/watch?v=HMExEWDv4Yc

Clarity Wellness Solutions. (2024, March 11). *10 Minute Chakra Healing Meditation* [Video]. YouTube. https://www.youtube.com/watch?v=zV-VrQyvUhQ

Clarity Wellness Solutions. (2024, Feb. 26). *15 Minute Meditation for Self-Love* [Video]. Youtube. https://www.youtube.com/watch?v=8P5oS2A7GsM

Clarity Wellness Solutions. (2023, Dec. 19). *20 Minute Guided Meditation to Reflect on Your Health Journey* [Video]. YouTube. https://www.youtube.com/watch?v=Xw0gJjEYgAE

Clarity Wellness Solutions. (2023, Sept. 21). *20 Minute Meditation for Anxiety* [Video]. YouTube. https://www.youtube.com/watch?v=0Ql97yE1BY4

Confucius. (2016, January 7). *The Great Learning: One of the "Four Books" in Confucianism.*

CreateSpace Independent Publishing Platform. https://www.amazon.com/Great-Learning-Four-Books-Confucianism/dp/1523294728

Dooley, M. & Leis K. & Tripoli, P. (Directors). (2012, March 1). *Thoughts Become Things* [Film;DVD]. Tut's Adventurer's Club. https://www.amazon.com/Thoughts-Become-Things-Mike-Dooley/dp/0981460224

Flender, R. (Director). (1999). *Idle Hands* [Film]. Columbia Pictures; Sony Pictures Releasing

Freud, S. (1962, January 1). *The Ego and the Id.* W.W. Norton Company. https://www.amazon.com/Ego-Id-Sigmund-Freud/dp/B0000CLI54

Gillespie, C. (2023, October 23). *What Is Generational Trauma?.* Health. https://www.health.com/condition/ptsd/generational-trauma

Goldsby, T. L., Goldsby, M. E., McWalters, M., & Mills, P. J. (2016). Effects of singing bowl sound meditation on mood, tension, and well-being: An observational study. *Journal of Evidence-Based Complementary & Alternative Medicine, 22*(3), 401–406. https://doi.org/10.1177/2156587216668109

Goldsmith, R. E., Gamache Martin, C., & Parnitzke Smith, C. (2014). Systemic trauma. *Journal of Trauma & Dissociation, 15*(2), 117–132. https://doi.org/10.1080/15299732.2014.871666

Goodreads. (n.d.). *A quote from living buddha, living christ.* Goodreads. https://www.goodreads.com/quotes/1345401-the-best-way-to-take-care-of-the-future-is

Harkins, P., Burke, E., Swales, C., & Silman, A. (2021). 'All Disease Begins in the Gut'—the Role of the Intestinal Microbiome in Ankylosing Spondylitis. *Rheumatology Advances in Practice, 5*(3). https://doi.org/10.1093/rap/rkab063

Herit, D. (Director). (2006). *The Secret* [Film]. Prime Time Productions. https://www.youtube.com/watch?v=Q6FXHAuptOI

Joel, B. (1977). Vienna [Song]. On *The Stranger* [Album]. Columbia Records.

Kabat-Zinn, J. (1994). *Wherever You Go, There You Are: Mindfulness Meditation in Everyday Life*. Hachette Books. https://www.amazon.com/Wherever-You-There-Are-Mindfulness/dp/1401307787

Linehan, M. (2014, October 20). *DBT Skills Training Manual: Second Edition*. The Guilford Press. https://a.co/d/aR9RHIn

McLeod, S. (2025, March 14). *Maslow's hierarchy of needs*. Simply Psychology. https://www.simplypsychology.org/maslow.html

Milligan, K., Calderon de la Bruca, L., & Kania, J. (2024, February 20). Guiding Questions to Identify Systemic Trauma. *Collective Change Lab*. https://www.collectivechangelab.org/blog/guiding-questions-to-identify-systemic-trauma

The Philosophy and Science of Mindfulness. Pursuit of Happiness. (2023, March 9). https://www.pursuit-of-happiness.org/science-of-happiness/positive-thinking/links-to-philosophy-of-mindfulness/

Pijanowski, B. C., Villanueva-Rivera, L. J., Dumyahn, S. L., Farina, A., Krause, B. L., Napoletano, B. M., Gage, S. H., & Pieretti, N. (2011). Soundscape ecology: The science of sound in the landscape. *BioScience, 61*(3), 203–216. https://doi.org/10.1525/bio.2011.61.3.6

Starkman, E., & Mitchell, K. (n.d.). *What is Reiki Therapy?* WebMD. https://www.webmd.com/pain-management/reiki-overview

Tolle, E. (2005). *A new earth: Awakening to your life's purpose*. Penguin Audio.

Tolle, E. (2007). *Living the liberated life and dealing with the pain-body*. Sounds True.

Trepp, B., & Sandweiss, D. (2023, September 18). *Mindful Movement: A Path to Holistic Well-Being*. Accelerate Learning Community. https://accelerate.uofuhealth.utah.edu/resilience/mindful-movement-a-path-to-holistic-well-being

U.S. Centers for Disease Control and Prevention. (2024, October 8). *About Adverse Childhood Experiences*. Centers for Disease Control and Prevention. https://www.cdc.gov/aces/about/index.html

U.S. Department of Health and Human Services. (n.d.-a). *Massage therapy: What you need to know*. National Center for Complementary and Integrative Health. https://www.nccih.nih.gov/health/massage-therapy-what-you-need-to-know

U.S. Department of Health and Human Services. (n.d.-b). *Yoga: Effectiveness and safety*. National Center for Complementary and Integrative Health. https://www.nccih.nih.gov/health/yoga-effectiveness-and-safety

U.S. Department of Health and Human Services. (n.d.). *Mental illness*. National Institute of Mental Health. https://www.nimh.nih.gov/health/statistics/mental-illness#part_2539

University of Rochester Medical Center. (n.d.). *Journaling for emotional wellness*. Journaling for Emotional Wellness. https://www.urmc.rochester.edu/encyclopedia/content?ContentID=4552&ContentTypeID=1

Vigderman, A., & Turner, G. (Eds.). (2024, May 30). *A Timeline of School Shootings since Columbine*. Security.org. https://www.security.org/blog/a-timeline-of-school-shootings-since-columbine/

Van der Kolk, B. (2015, September 24.). *The body keeps the score: Brain, mind, and body in the healing of trauma: Amazon.co.uk: Kolk, Bessel van der: 9780141978611: Books*. Amazon. https://www.amazon.co.uk/Body-Keeps-Score-Transformation-Trauma/dp/0141978619

Workshops & Series. Mary Pinkard. (n.d.). https://www.marypinkard.com/workshops-series

www.ingramcontent.com/pod-product-compliance
Lightning Source LLC
Chambersburg PA
CBHW051315120626
46547CB00015B/2240